The Australian Women's Weekly
cookbooks

It seems just like yesterday we all thought Thai food was terribly exotic and its ingredients difficult to find. Nowadays, we're as likely to be cooking Thai for dinner as we are Italian or Indian, and most of its ingredients can be found without hassle at the local supermarket. One of the reasons (besides the fact that it's delicious!) we've embraced this cuisine so wholeheartedly is because it suits today's lifestyle: it's easy and quick to prepare, and its emphasis on fresh ingredients treated simply keeps step with our desire for healthy eating.

Pamela Clark

Food Director

contents

Wash and thoroughly dry the coriander before starting to chop the root

Use kitchen scissors to cut the soaked and drained vermicelli into random short lengths

Spoon a level teaspoon of filling near one corner of each wrapper then roll, tucking in the ends

spring rolls   poh pia tod

PREPARATION TIME 20 MINUTES **COOKING TIME** 20 MINUTES (PLUS REFRIGERATION TIME)

20g rice vermicelli

2 teaspoons peanut oil

100g pork mince

1 clove garlic, crushed

1 fresh small red thai chilli, chopped finely

1 green onion, chopped finely

1 small carrot (70g), grated finely

1 teaspoon finely chopped coriander root and stem mixture

1 teaspoon fish sauce

50g shelled cooked prawns, chopped finely

1 teaspoon cornflour

2 teaspoons water

12 x 12cm-square spring roll wrappers

vegetable oil, for deep-frying

CUCUMBER DIPPING SAUCE

1 lebanese cucumber, seeded, sliced thinly

½ cup (110g) sugar

1 cup (250ml) water

½ cup (125ml) white vinegar

1 tablespoon grated fresh ginger

1 teaspoon salt

2 fresh small red thai chillies, sliced thinly

3 green onions, sliced thinly

1 tablespoon coarsely chopped fresh coriander

1 Place vermicelli in medium heatproof bowl; cover with boiling water. Stand until just tender; drain. Using kitchen scissors, cut vermicelli into random lengths.

2 Heat oil in wok; stir-fry pork, garlic and chilli until pork is changed in colour. Add onion, carrot, coriander mixture, fish sauce and prawns; stir-fry until vegetables just soften. Place stir-fried mixture in small bowl with vermicelli; cool.

3 Blend cornflour with the water in small bowl. Place 1 level tablespoon of the filling near one corner of each wrapper. Lightly brush edges of each wrapper with cornflour mixture; roll to enclose filling, folding in ends.

4 Make dipping sauce (freeze excess for a future use).

5 Just before serving, heat oil in wok or large saucepan; deep-fry spring rolls, in batches, until golden brown. Drain on absorbent paper; serve with cucumber dipping sauce.

cucumber dipping sauce Place cucumber in heatproof serving bowl. Combine sugar, the water, vinegar, ginger and salt in small saucepan, stir over heat without boiling until sugar is dissolved; pour over cucumber. Sprinkle with chilli, onion and coriander; refrigerate, covered, until chilled.

MAKES 12 SPRING ROLLS AND 1½ CUPS DIPPING SAUCE
per spring roll 3.5g fat; 279kJ (67 cal)
per tablespoon dipping sauce 0g fat; 107kJ (26 cal)

You need to cook and mash a medium potato weighing about 200g for this recipe

Using a 9cm cutter, you'll be able to cut four rounds from each sheet of puff pastry

Fold the puff pastry over to enclose the filling, pressing the edges together to seal

curry puffs kari puff

PREPARATION TIME 30 MINUTES **COOKING TIME** 35 MINUTES

2 teaspoons peanut oil
2 teaspoons finely chopped coriander root
2 green onions, chopped finely
1 clove garlic, crushed
100g beef mince
½ teaspoon ground turmeric
½ teaspoon ground cumin
¼ teaspoon ground coriander
2 teaspoons fish sauce
1 tablespoon water
½ cup (110g) mashed potato
2 sheets ready-rolled frozen puff pastry
1 egg, beaten lightly
vegetable oil, for deep frying

SWEET CHILLI DIPPING SAUCE
12 fresh small red thai chillies, chopped coarsely
8 cloves garlic, quartered
2 cups (500ml) white vinegar
1 cup (220g) caster sugar
2 teaspoons salt
2 teaspoons tamarind paste

1 Make dipping sauce (freeze excess for a future use).
2 Heat oil in wok; stir-fry coriander root, onion, garlic and beef until beef is changed in colour. Add turmeric, cumin and ground coriander; stir-fry until fragrant. Add fish sauce and the water; simmer, uncovered, until mixture thickens. Stir in potato; cool.
3 Using 9cm cutter, cut four rounds from each pastry sheet. Place 1 level tablespoon of the filling in centre of each round; brush around edge lightly with egg. Fold pastry over to enclose filling, pressing edges together to seal.
4 Just before serving, heat oil in large saucepan; deep-fry curry puffs, in batches, until crisp and browned lightly. Drain on absorbent paper; serve with dipping sauce.
sweet chilli dipping sauce Place ingredients in medium saucepan, stir over heat without boiling until sugar is dissolved; bring to a boil. Reduce heat; simmer, uncovered, about 20 minutes or until slightly thickened. Cool 5 minutes; blend or process until pureed.

MAKES 8 CURRY PUFFS AND 1½ CUPS DIPPING SAUCE
per curry puff 8.3g fat; 481kJ (115 cal)
per tablespoon dipping sauce 0g fat; 220kJ (52 cal)

TIPS

● Do not use instant mashed potato.
● Make a vegetarian version of this recipe by omitting the mince and using either 1 cup of finely shredded cabbage or 100g of finely chopped tofu instead.
● Filling mixture can be made a day ahead and kept, covered, under refrigeration until you want to make the curry puffs. You can freeze the cooked puffs once they have cooled. Just before serving, place on a metal rack over an oven tray and reheat in a preheated moderate oven for about 15 minutes or until crisp and heated through.

● Make sure the oil is very hot before deep-frying the curry puffs, and try not to crowd them in the pan or they will cook unevenly. Turn them constantly using a metal slotted spoon, and keep them warm on an absorbent-paper-lined oven tray in a very slow oven.

Stack pairs of the wrappers with the top one on a diagonal to form star shape

Using a sharp knife, cut the top half of each green onion lengthways into four long strips

Wrap the strips of onion around the neck of the pouches and secure them with toothpicks

money bags   tung tong

PREPARATION TIME 30 MINUTES   **COOKING TIME** 20 MINUTES

1 tablespoon peanut oil
1 small brown onion (80g), chopped finely
1 clove garlic, crushed
1 tablespoon grated fresh ginger
100g chicken mince
1 tablespoon finely grated palm sugar
1 tablespoon finely chopped roasted
   unsalted peanuts
2 teaspoons finely chopped fresh coriander
3 green onions
24 x 8cm-square wonton wrappers
vegetable oil, for deep-frying

PEANUT DIPPING SAUCE
1 tablespoon peanut oil
2 cloves garlic, crushed
1 small brown onion (80g), chopped finely
2 fresh small red chillies, seeded,
   chopped coarsely
1 stick fresh lemon grass, chopped finely
¾ cup (180ml) coconut milk
2 tablespoons fish sauce
¼ cup firmly packed dark brown sugar
½ cup (140g) crunchy peanut butter
½ teaspoon curry powder
1 tablespoon lime juice

1 Heat oil in wok; stir-fry onion, garlic and ginger until onion softens. Add chicken; stir-fry until chicken is changed in colour. Add sugar; stir-fry about 3 minutes or until sugar dissolves. Stir nuts and coriander into filling mixture.
2 Cut upper green half of each onion into four long slices; discard remaining onion half. Submerge onion strips in hot water for a few seconds to make pliable.
3 Place 12 wrappers on board; cover each wrapper with another, placed on the diagonal to form star shape. Place rounded teaspoons of the filling mixture in centre of each star; gather corners to form pouch shape. Tie green onion slice around neck of each pouch to hold closed, secure with toothpick.
4 Make dipping sauce (freeze excess for a future use).
5 Just before serving, heat oil in wok or large saucepan; deep-fry money bags, in batches, until crisp and browned lightly. Drain on absorbent paper; serve with peanut dipping sauce.
   peanut dipping sauce Heat oil in small saucepan; cook garlic and onion until softened. Stir in remaining ingredients; bring to a boil. Reduce heat; simmer, stirring, about 2 minutes or until sauce thickens.

MAKES 12 MONEY BAGS AND 1½ CUPS DIPPING SAUCE
per money bag 5.1g fat; 425kJ (101 cal)
per tablespoon dipping sauce 7g fat; 378kJ (90 cal)

Immerse bamboo skewers in water before use to prevent them from splintering as you thread on the meat

Keep meat towards one end of skewers so you have something to hold onto when turning them

Bring coconut milk to a boil before adding remainder of the ingredients for the satay sauce

mixed satay sticks   satay gai, nuah, muu

PREPARATION TIME 20 MINUTES (PLUS MARINATING TIME)   **COOKING TIME** 15 MINUTES

250g chicken breast fillets
250g beef eye fillet
250g pork fillet
2 cloves garlic, crushed
2 teaspoons brown sugar
¼ teaspoon sambal oelek
1 teaspoon ground turmeric
¼ teaspoon curry powder
½ teaspoon ground cumin
½ teaspoon ground coriander
2 tablespoons peanut oil

SATAY SAUCE
½ cup (80g) roasted unsalted peanuts
2 tablespoons red curry paste (page 112)
¾ cup (180ml) coconut milk
¼ cup (60ml) chicken stock (page 117)
1 tablespoon kaffir lime juice
1 tablespoon brown sugar

1 Cut chicken, beef and pork into long 1.5cm-thick strips; thread strips onto skewers. Place skewers, in single layer, on tray or in shallow baking dish; brush with combined garlic, sugar, sambal, spices and oil. Cover; refrigerate 3 hours or overnight.
2 Make satay sauce.
3 Cook skewers on heated oiled grill plate (or grill or barbecue) until browned all over and cooked as desired. Serve immediately with satay sauce.
   satay sauce Blend or process nuts until chopped finely; add paste, process until just combined. Bring coconut milk to a boil in small saucepan; add peanut mixture, whisking until smooth. Reduce heat, add stock; cook, stirring, about 3 minutes or until sauce thickens slightly. Add juice and sugar, stirring, until sugar dissolves.

MAKES 12 SKEWERS AND 1¼ CUPS SATAY SAUCE
per skewer 6.1g fat; 471kJ (112 cal)
per tablespoon satay sauce 5.5g fat; 278kJ (66 cal)

TIPS

● You need 12 bamboo skewers for this recipe. Soak the skewers in water for at least an hour before threading the meat onto them to help keep them from splintering or scorching. If a bamboo skewer does start to char, wrap a folded piece of foil around it to protect it.

● Skewers for various recipes can be made from sticks of lemon grass, sugar cane, rosemary and even cinnamon – let the recipe's ingredients dictate a harmonious choice of skewer.
● Vegetables and tofu can also be skewered, either with the meats or on their own.

● Skewers of meat and chicken can be brushed with combined garlic, spices and oil a day ahead and refrigerated, covered, until required. They can also be frozen for up to a month.
● Grate the kaffir lime before juicing it and freeze the rind in a tightly sealed plastic bag. You can substitute the kaffir with an ordinary lime if necessary.

After removing any skin or bones, cut the fish into small pieces

Cut the trimmed snake beans into very small, paper-thin pieces before mixing with fish

Roll heaped tablespoons of the fish mixture into balls, then flatten into cake shapes with your fingers

fish cakes   tod mun pla

PREPARATION TIME 15 MINUTES   **COOKING TIME** 10 MINUTES

500g redfish fillets, skinned and boned
2 tablespoons red curry paste (page 112)
2 fresh kaffir lime leaves, torn
2 green onions, chopped coarsely
1 tablespoon fish sauce
1 tablespoon lime juice
2 tablespoons finely chopped fresh coriander
3 snake beans (30g), chopped finely
2 fresh small red thai chillies, chopped finely
peanut oil, for deep-frying

1 Cut fish into small pieces. Blend or process fish with curry paste, lime leaves, onion, sauce and juice until mixture forms a smooth paste. Combine fish mixture in medium bowl with coriander, beans and chilli.

2 Roll heaped tablespoon of the fish mixture into ball, then flatten into cake shape; repeat with remaining mixture.

3 Just before serving, heat oil in wok or large saucepan; deep-fry fish cakes, in batches, until browned lightly and cooked through. Drain on absorbent paper; serve with fresh coriander leaves and lime wedges, if desired.

MAKES 16 FISH CAKES
per fish cake 2.8g fat; 201kJ (48 cal)

TIPS

● These fish cakes are good served with cucumber dipping sauce (page 4) and a small mound of grated carrot on the side, if you prefer.
● We used red fish fillets for this recipe but you can use any boneless, mild, sweet-tasting, slightly firm white fish fillet – flathead or flake are also good choices of fish to make the cakes.
● Check for any small pieces of bone in the fillets and use tweezers to remove them. Salting your fingers helps you get a better grip when pulling away any remaining skin from the fish.

● Dip your fingers in cold water when shaping the fish cakes to prevent the mixture sticking; flatten the cakes until they are about 5cm in diameter and 2.5cm thick. Placing the uncooked fish cakes on a plastic-wrap-lined tray and refrigerating them for about an hour will firm them and help ensure they don't fall apart during cooking.
● Uncooked fish cakes can be shaped a day ahead and kept, covered, overnight in the refrigerator.

● Make certain the oil is hot before you start frying the fish cakes, and try not to crowd them in the pan or they will cook unevenly. Turn them once, and keep the finished fish cakes warm by placing them on an absorbent-paper-lined oven tray in a very slow oven while you finish deep-frying the remainder.
● Fish cakes can also be sprayed on one side with cooking-oil spray and char-grilled, oiled-side down, on the flat-plate of a barbecue for about 2 minutes. Spray uncooked side, then turn and cook a further 2 minutes.

Use a mortar and pestle to pulverise the dried green peppercorns into a powder

Chopping the lemon grass as finely as possible will release its full flavour into the marinade

After slicing the carrot into long matchsticks, immerse in iced water so that they remain crisp

crying tiger seur rong hai

PREPARATION TIME 20 MINUTES (PLUS MARINATING TIME) **COOKING TIME** 10 MINUTES (PLUS STANDING TIME)

50g dried tamarind

1 cup (250ml) boiling water

400g beef eye fillet

2 cloves garlic, crushed

2 teaspoons dried green peppercorns, crushed

1 tablespoon peanut oil

2 tablespoons fish sauce

2 tablespoons soy sauce

1 stick fresh lemon grass, chopped finely

2 fresh small red thai chillies, chopped finely

1 large carrot (180g)

1 cup (80g) thinly sliced chinese cabbage

CRYING TIGER SAUCE

¼ cup (60ml) fish sauce

¼ cup (60ml) lime juice

2 teaspoons grated palm sugar

1 teaspoon finely chopped dried red thai chilli

1 green onion, sliced thinly

2 teaspoons finely chopped fresh coriander

reserved tamarind pulp (see step 1)

1 Soak tamarind in the water for 30 minutes. Pour tamarind into a fine strainer set over a small bowl; push as much tamarind pulp through the strainer as possible, scraping underside of strainer occasionally. Discard any tamarind solids left in strainer; reserve ½ cup of pulp for the crying tiger sauce.

2 Halve beef lengthways. Combine remaining tamarind pulp, garlic, peppercorns, oil, sauces, lemon grass and chilli in large bowl; add beef, stir to coat beef all over in marinade. Cover; refrigerate 3 hours or overnight.

3 Make crying tiger sauce.

4 Cook beef on heated oiled grill plate (or grill or barbecue) about 10 minutes or until browned all over and cooked as desired. Cover beef; stand 10 minutes, slice thinly.

5 Meanwhile, cut carrot into 10cm lengths; slice each length thinly, cut slices into thin matchsticks.

6 Place sliced beef on serving dish with carrot and cabbage; serve crying tiger sauce separately.
   crying tiger sauce Combine ingredients in small bowl; whisk until sugar dissolves.

SERVES 4
per serving 10.9g fat; 951kJ (227 cal)

TIPS

● Bangkok's famous seur rong hai's spicy flavour is supposed to be hot enough to make even a tiger cry, but the lemon grass, green peppercorns and tamarind help balance the heat with their typically Thai blend of sweet-sour flavours.

● When you use fresh lemon grass, start chopping from the white end, going up only until you just reach the green upper part of the stalk. Discard the tough top green section. Lemon or lime rind can be substituted for the lemon grass in this recipe.

● When cutting the carrot into matchsticks, use the top half of the peeled carrot for consistent size. Chilling the matchsticks by immersing them in a bowl of iced water makes them crisp and crunchy.

Cut the lemon grass into tiny pieces, starting from the white end of the stalk

Using a large sharp knife, chop the cleaned crab body into quarters, leaving the claws intact

Dried chillies can be pulverised with a mortar and pestle instead of chopping them with a knife

spicy seafood soup   poh taek

PREPARATION TIME 20 MINUTES **COOKING TIME** 15 MINUTES

1 medium uncooked blue swimmer crab (500g)
150g firm white fish fillets
8 medium black mussels (200g)
150g squid hoods
1.25 litres (5 cups) chicken stock (page 117)
2 sticks fresh lemon grass, chopped finely
20g piece fresh galangal, sliced thinly
4 fresh kaffir lime leaves
6 fresh small green thai chillies,
   chopped coarsely
4 dried long red thai chillies, chopped finely
8 large uncooked prawns (400g)
1 teaspoon grated palm sugar
2 tablespoons fish sauce
1 tablespoon lime juice
¼ cup fresh thai basil leaves

1 Remove and discard back shell and gills of crab; rinse under cold water. Chop crab body into quarters, leaving claws intact. Cut fish into bite-sized portions; scrub mussels, remove beards. Cut squid into 2cm-thick slices; score the inside in a diagonal pattern.

2 Combine chicken stock, lemon grass, galangal, lime leaves and both chillies in large saucepan; bring to a boil.

3 Add prepared seafood and unshelled prawns to boiling stock mixture; cook, uncovered, about 5 minutes or until seafood is just cooked through. Remove from heat; stir in remaining ingredients. Serve hot.

SERVES 4
per serving 2.8g fat; 815kJ (195 cal)

TIPS

● This classic Bangkok floating market hot and sour mixed seafood soup is, like a cioppino, bouillabaisse or mongolian hot pot, almost a meal in itself and, indeed, in Thailand it is often served with steamed rice as a main course. Its singularly clean citrus-like flavour is attributable to the inclusion of fairly large amounts of kaffir lime leaves, galangal and lemon grass.

● Galangal is a rhizome with a hot ginger-citrusy flavour and is used similarly to ginger and garlic as a seasoning. Sometimes known as thai, siamese or laos ginger, it also comes in a dried powdered form called laos. Fresh ginger can be substituted for galangal if you cannot find it.

● The dried chillies in this recipe can be crushed to a more powdery consistency by using a mortar and pestle.
● When you use fresh lemon grass, start chopping from the white end, going up only until you just reach the green upper part of the stalk. Discard the tough top green section. Lemon or lime rind can be substituted for the lemon grass in this recipe.

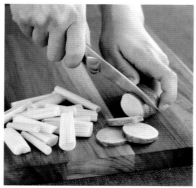

Galangal and lemon grass are strained out of the soup so you don't have to chop them finely

Whole fresh kaffir lime leaves are added to the stock mixture at the start of cooking

Rinse the straw mushrooms in a sieve under cold water to remove any traces of the can liquid

chicken and galangal soup   tom ka gai

PREPARATION TIME 15 MINUTES (PLUS STANDING TIME) **COOKING TIME** 35 MINUTES

3 cups (750ml) chicken stock (page 117)
20g fresh galangal, sliced thickly
2 sticks fresh lemon grass, cut into 5cm pieces
4 fresh kaffir lime leaves
2 teaspoons coarsely chopped coriander root
　and stem mixture
500g chicken thigh fillets, sliced thinly
200g drained canned straw mushrooms, rinsed
1 cup (250ml) coconut milk
1 tablespoon lime juice
1 tablespoon fish sauce
1 teaspoon grated palm sugar
¼ cup loosely packed fresh coriander leaves
2 fresh small red thai chillies, seeded,
　sliced thinly
2 fresh kaffir lime leaves, shredded
1 stick fresh lemon grass, sliced thinly

1 Combine stock, galangal, lemon grass pieces, whole lime leaves and coriander mixture in large saucepan; bring to a boil. Reduce heat; simmer, covered, 5 minutes. Remove from heat; stand 10 minutes. Strain stock through muslin into large heatproof bowl; discard solids.

2 Return stock to same cleaned pan. Add chicken and mushrooms; bring to a boil. Reduce heat; simmer, uncovered, about 5 minutes or until chicken is cooked through. Stir in coconut milk, juice, sauce and sugar; cook, stirring, until just heated through (do not allow to boil). Remove from heat; stir in coriander leaves, chilli, shredded lime leaves and lemon grass slices. Serve hot.

SERVES 4
per serving 22.8g fat; 1398kJ (334 cal)

TIPS

● Tom (broth or stock), ka (fresh galangal) and gai (chicken) come together in this popular Thai soup that is more subtle and smoother than its fiery counterpart, tom yum goong, thanks to the moderating effect of the added coconut milk.
● Coconut milk should be refrigerated after using the single cup called for here; it will keep for up to a week. We do not suggest that you freeze leftover

coconut milk because it increases the likelihood of curdling when the thawed milk is used in cooking. Avoid buying cans of sweetened coconut milk – it is not recommended for Thai cooking.
● Both the stems and roots of coriander are used here, so be certain to buy a bunch of fresh coriander having its roots intact. Wash the coriander under cold water, removing any dirt clinging to the roots.

● Galangal is a rhizome (a knob-like underground-growing stem) having a hot ginger-citrusy flavour. It is used similarly to ginger and garlic – fresh as an ingredient, or dried and ground as a seasoning.
● Cut the two fresh lemon grass sticks into 5cm-long pieces, then, using the side of a heavy knife, pound the pieces: bruising them this way helps release flavour into the soup.

Stack kaffir lime leaves and roll into cigar shape before shredding finely

Stir the prawn heads and shells in pan over high heat until they turn deep orange in colour

Grate the fresh ginger on the medium-size holes of a four-side grater just before adding to soup

spicy sour prawn soup   tom yum goong

PREPARATION TIME 20 MINUTES   **COOKING TIME** 40 MINUTES

900g large uncooked king prawns
1 tablespoon peanut oil
1.5 litres (6 cups) water
2 tablespoons red curry paste (page 112)
1 tablespoon tamarind concentrate
2 tablespoons finely chopped fresh lemon grass
1 teaspoon ground turmeric
2 fresh small red thai chillies, seeded, chopped coarsely
1 tablespoon grated fresh ginger
6 fresh kaffir lime leaves, shredded finely
1 teaspoon grated palm sugar
100g shiitake mushrooms, halved
2 tablespoons fish sauce
2 tablespoons lime juice
¼ cup loosely packed fresh vietnamese mint leaves
¼ cup loosely packed fresh coriander leaves

1 Shell and devein prawns, leaving tails intact.
2 Heat oil in large saucepan; cook prawn shells and heads, stirring, about 5 minutes or until shells and heads are deep orange in colour.
3 Add 1 cup of the water and curry paste to pan; bring to a boil, stirring. Add remaining water; return to a boil. Reduce heat; simmer, uncovered, 20 minutes. Strain stock through muslin into large heatproof bowl; discard solids.
4 Return stock to same cleaned pan. Add tamarind, lemon grass, turmeric, chilli, ginger, lime leaves and sugar; bring to a boil. Boil, stirring, 2 minutes. Reduce heat; add mushrooms; cook, stirring, 3 minutes. Add prawns; cook, stirring, until prawns are changed in colour. Remove from heat; stir in sauce and juice. Serve soup hot, topped with mint and coriander.

SERVES 4
per serving 7.6g fat; 781kJ (187 cal)

TIPS

● Tom yums are the most popular soups in Thailand and very well known among Thai food lovers around the world. Translated loosely as broth or stock (tom) and combined spicy sour (yum), this soup is far more complex than the name would indicate. This version, made with prawns, is probably the one most favoured by Westerners. Sour and tangy, without that cloying sweetness

coconut milk adds to other soups, tom yum goong's unique taste comes from the combination of spicy ingredients, like chilli and curry paste, with sour ones, such as lime juice and tamarind.
● You will need about 2 medium limes for this recipe.
● When cutting the lemon grass, chop from the white end, going up only until you reach the lower green part.

● Vietnamese mint is not a mint at all, but a pungent and peppery narrow-leafed member of the buckwheat family. Nor is its use confined to Vietnam: it is also called cambodian mint, pak pai (Thailand), laksa leaf (Indonesia), daun kesom (Singapore)… and rau ram in Vietnam! It is a common ingredient in Thai foods, particularly soups, salads and stir-fries.

Use the rim of the bowl of a small spoon to scrape away the skin from the ginger

Stir the tamarind concentrate into the boiling water in a heatproof jug until it dissolves

Chop the pickled garlic bulb finely without separating the cloves or removing the peel

pork and pickled garlic green curry
gaeng hang leh muu

PREPARATION TIME 20 MINUTES (PLUS MARINATING TIME) **COOKING TIME** 20 MINUTES

¼ cup (35g) coarsely chopped fresh ginger

3 cloves garlic, quartered

1 medium brown onion (150g), chopped coarsely

1 teaspoon ground turmeric

2 tablespoons green curry paste (page 112)

10 fresh kaffir lime leaves, torn

750g pork fillet, cut into 2cm cubes

¼ cup (60ml) peanut oil

1 tablespoon tamarind concentrate

1 cup (250ml) boiling water

2 tablespoons fish sauce

2 bulbs pickled garlic (50g), drained, chopped coarsely

2 teaspoons grated palm sugar

1 Process or blend ginger, fresh garlic, onion, turmeric, curry paste and half of the lime leaves until mixture is almost smooth; combine in large bowl with pork. Toss to coat pork all over in marinade, cover; refrigerate at least 30 minutes.

2 Heat oil in large saucepan; cook pork mixture, stirring, until lightly browned all over.

3 Meanwhile, blend tamarind with the water in small jug; stir in fish sauce. Add tamarind mixture to pan; cook, uncovered, about 10 minutes or until pork is tender.

4 Add pickled garlic and sugar; simmer, stirring occasionally, about 5 minutes or until sauce thickens slightly.

5 Place curry in serving bowl; sprinkle with finely shredded remaining kaffir lime leaves.

SERVES 4
per serving 21.2g fat; 1650kJ (394 cal)

TIPS

● We suggest that the curries in this chapter be accompanied by steamed jasmine rice (page 67).

● Called a northern Thai curry because it's a favourite of the residents of Chiang Mai, this curry is best made a day ahead so that the flavours can develop fully.

● There are two basic types of curry, one made with coconut cream or milk, and the other water- or stock-based. A "wet" curry such as this one is often dominantly sour in flavour, from the tamarind as well as the kaffir lime leaves used in making the sauce, and because there is no added coconut.

● Kaffir lime leaves are readily available from most greengrocers and many supermarkets; if you can't get fresh, it's acceptable to used dried.

● Ginger used in a marinade doesn't necessarily have to be peeled if it is young (without many knobs and fairly smooth-skinned). However, it's easy to peel a small amount of ginger by using the rim of the bowl of a small spoon to scrape away the skin.

● Sweet and subtle pickled garlic, or kratiem dong, is the young green bulb, packed whole and unpeeled in vinegar brine. Eaten as a snack in Thailand, it can be served as a condiment to be sprinkled over noodle or rice dishes or can be used in cooking.

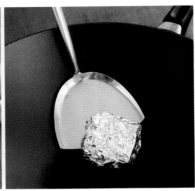

Remove stems, then quarter thai eggplants before removing their bitter seeds

Slice approximately a teaspoon of shrimp paste off the block, then wrap it tightly in foil

Quickly toss the foil package of shrimp paste in a hot wok until it is fragrant and feels slightly soft

seafood and thai eggplant yellow curry
gaeng leuang taleh

PREPARATION TIME 30 MINUTES **COOKING TIME** 30 MINUTES

500g squid hoods
400g firm white fish fillets
8 medium uncooked prawns (200g)
8 medium black mussels (200g)
12 scallops (240g)
1 teaspoon shrimp paste
1 tablespoon peanut oil
2 tablespoons yellow curry paste (page 113)
2 cloves garlic, crushed
2 teaspoons grated fresh ginger
1 medium brown onion (150g), sliced thickly
1 stick fresh lemon grass, chopped finely
1 fresh long red thai chilli, chopped coarsely
12 fresh thai eggplants (350g), quartered
1 cup (250ml) fish stock (page 117)
400ml can coconut milk
3 fresh kaffir lime leaves, torn
1 tablespoon grated palm sugar
½ cup firmly packed fresh coriander leaves
2 tablespoons lime juice
2 fresh long red thai chillies, sliced thinly

1 Cut squid into 1.5cm slices and fish into 3cm pieces; shell and devein prawns, leaving tails intact. Scrub mussels; remove beards. Remove and discard any scallop roe.

2 Wrap shrimp paste in foil, place in heated wok or large saucepan; roast, tossing, until fragrant. Discard foil, return shrimp paste to same heated pan with oil and curry paste; stir over heat until blended.

3 Add garlic, ginger, onion, lemon grass and chopped chilli; cook, stirring, until onion softens. Add eggplant; cook, stirring, 2 minutes. Add stock, coconut milk, lime leaves and sugar; bring to a boil. Reduce heat; simmer, stirring occasionally, 10 minutes.

4 Add fish; cook, uncovered, 3 minutes. Add remaining seafood; cook, covered, about 5 minutes or until prawns change colour and mussels open (discard any that do not). Stir in coriander and juice.

5 Place curry in serving bowl; sprinkle with sliced chilli and coriander leaves, if desired.

SERVES 4
per serving 32.5g fat; 2691kJ (643 cal)

TIPS

● Shrimp paste, also known as khapi, trasi or blanchan, is a strong-smelling, fairly solid paste made of salted dried shrimp. It should be chopped or sliced thinly, then wrapped in foil and roasted before use.

● Thai eggplants, makeua prao, are golf-ball-size eggplants available in different colours, but most commonly green traced in off-white. They're crunchier than purple Western eggplants, and their seeds should be removed because they're quite bitter.

● Buy scallops without roe and calamari rings, if you like, to cut back on the preparation time. You can prepare all of the seafood early in the day and keep it, covered, under refrigeration until you're ready to make the curry.

Use poultry or kitchen scissors to cut the barbecued duck into 12 even-size pieces

Pack unchopped thai basil leaves into a ⅓-cup measure after removing them from stems

Stirring the curry mixture constantly while bringing it to a boil helps prevent it separating

duck red curry gaeng ped pet yang

PREPARATION TIME 15 MINUTES **COOKING TIME** 15 MINUTES

¼ cup (75g) red curry paste (page 112)
400ml can coconut milk
½ cup (125ml) chicken stock (page 117)
2 fresh kaffir lime leaves, torn
1 tablespoon fish sauce
1 tablespoon lime juice
⅓ cup firmly packed fresh thai basil leaves
1 whole barbecued duck (1kg),
   cut into 12 pieces
565g can lychees, rinsed, drained
225g can bamboo shoots, rinsed, drained
3 fresh long red thai chillies, sliced thinly

1 Place curry paste in large saucepan; stir over heat until fragrant. Add coconut milk, stock, lime leaves, sauce and juice; bring to a boil. Reduce heat; simmer, stirring, 5 minutes.
2 Reserve about eight small whole basil leaves for garnish; add remaining basil leaves with duck, lychees and bamboo shoots to curry mixture. Cook, stirring occasionally, about 5 minutes or until heated through.
3 Place curry in serving bowl; sprinkle with sliced chilli and reserved thai basil leaves.

SERVES 4
per serving 47.2g fat; 2408kJ (575 cal)

TIPS

● Western food has two primary tastes: sweet and salty. South-East Asian food in general and Thai in particular is far more complex, having four distinct tastes – sweet, salty, spicy, sour – and a less dominant fifth, bitter. Nowhere do these different flavours meet and blend more harmoniously than in Thai curries such as this one, a perfect amalgam of sweet (coconut), salty (fish sauce), spicy (red curry paste) and sour (kaffir lime).
● You can roast a whole raw duck for this recipe if you wish, but it's simpler to purchase a large barbecued duck from your local Asian barbecued meat shop. Another alternative is to buy 750g of

raw duck breast fillets (about 5 fillets); chop them coarsely and stir-fry until they're browned before adding them to the curry mixture.
● Using kitchen scissors to separate the duck pieces is easier than trying to cut them up with a knife, and it helps keep the various pieces uniform in size too.
● If fresh lychees are in season when you make this curry, use them in preference to the canned version. A dozen fresh lychees, peeled, halved and seeded, will be sufficient.
● Your favourite kind of chilli can be used in this recipe because it is simply sprinkled over the top of the finished

curry as a garnish. Green or yellow chilli varieties make interesting alternatives to the red. If you seed these chillies, make sure you wear disposable kitchen gloves because the seeds and membranes can burn your skin.
● When you bring the curry paste mixture to a boil, don't cover the pan or the contents will boil over. Stirring constantly will assist with incorporating the curry paste into the coconut milk thoroughly and helps prevent the mixture from "separating" (stops the oil in the coconut milk leaching out and forming a layer of greasy beads on the surface of the curry).

Trim excess fat off the chicken thigh fillets, then cut into quarters on the diagonal

Use your fingers to pull the individual eggplants from their stalk before quartering them

Rolling a room-temperature lime on a hard surface, pressing down firmly, makes juicing it easier

chicken green curry gaeng keow wahn gai

PREPARATION TIME 20 MINUTES **COOKING TIME** 20 MINUTES

¼ cup (75g) green curry paste (page 112)
2 x 400ml cans coconut milk
2 fresh kaffir lime leaves, torn
1kg chicken thigh fillets
2 tablespoons peanut oil
2 tablespoons fish sauce
2 tablespoons lime juice
1 tablespoon grated palm sugar
150g pea eggplants, quartered
1 small zucchini (150g), cut into 5cm pieces
⅓ cup loosely packed fresh thai basil leaves
¼ cup coarsely chopped fresh coriander
1 tablespoon fresh coriander leaves
1 fresh long green thai chilli, sliced thinly
2 green onions, sliced thinly

1 Place curry paste in large saucepan; stir over heat until fragrant. Add coconut milk and lime leaves; bring to a boil. Reduce heat; simmer, stirring, 5 minutes.

2 Meanwhile, quarter chicken pieces. Heat oil in large frying pan; cook chicken, in batches, until just browned. Drain on absorbent paper.

3 Add chicken to curry mixture with sauce, juice, sugar and eggplants; simmer, covered, about 5 minutes or until eggplants are tender and chicken is cooked through. Add zucchini, basil and chopped coriander; cook, stirring, until zucchini is just tender.

4 Place curry in serving bowl; sprinkle with coriander leaves, sliced chilli and onion.

SERVES 4
per serving 72.4g fat; 3826kJ (914 cal)

TIPS

● Remove any fat from the chicken thigh fillets before cutting them. You can substitute chicken breast fillets but you'll find that the thighs' more distinctive flavour stands up to the robustness of the curry.
● Roll a room-temperature lime, pressing down on it firmly, on your kitchen bench. This helps release the juice from inside the pulp.

● Traditionally, the chicken is not cooked separately first, as we have done, but simply poached in the curry sauce. Not only does this result in the curry having a higher fat content but the chicken fat can make the finished dish look somewhat greasy or even curdled. Discarding the fat left in the pan after browning the chicken will have no effect on the flavour of the curry.

● Pea eggplants, makeua puong, can be found in Asian supermarkets and specialist greengrocers. They are a bit larger than green peas, have a distinctive, almost bitter, taste and come attached to stalks in clusters, like grapes. Snip them off the stalk with kitchen scissors. They can be substituted with an equal weight of thai eggplants or, if all else fails, fresh shelled peas.

Pick over the fish and remove any traces of bone with tweezers before cutting it

Palm sugar can be coarsely grated using the largest holes on a four-side grater

Boiling the coconut milk until it reduces brings the oil content to the surface

fish and potato yellow curry gaeng leuang pla

PREPARATION TIME 20 MINUTES **COOKING TIME** 20 MINUTES

8 tiny new potatoes (320g), halved
400ml can coconut milk
2 tablespoons yellow curry paste (page 113)
¼ cup (60ml) fish stock (page 117)
2 tablespoons fish sauce
1 tablespoon lime juice
1 tablespoon grated palm sugar
800g firm white fish fillets, cut into 3cm pieces
4 green onions, sliced thinly
⅓ cup coarsely chopped fresh coriander
1 fresh long red thai chilli, seeded, sliced thinly
1 tablespoon fresh coriander leaves

1 Boil, steam or microwave potato until almost tender; drain.
2 Meanwhile, place half of the coconut milk in large saucepan; bring to a boil. Boil, stirring, until reduced by half and the oil has separated from the coconut milk. Add curry paste; cook, stirring, about 1 minute or until fragrant. Add remaining coconut milk, stock, sauce, juice and sugar; cook, stirring, until sugar dissolves.
3 Add fish and potato to pan; cook, stirring occasionally, about 3 minutes or until fish is cooked as desired. Stir in onion and chopped coriander.
4 Place curry in serving bowl; sprinkle with sliced chilli and coriander leaves.

SERVES 4
per serving 24.2g fat; 2004kJ (479 cal)

TIPS

● Yellow curry paste is one of the mildest pastes and is the one that most closely resembles an Indian curry because of the inclusion of turmeric. This particular fish curry, too, is similar to many of the curries found on the west coast of India, those from Goa or Kerala, areas from which many traders ventured east to Thailand, taking with them a host of cultural and culinary influences.
● Boiling half of the coconut milk down so that much of the watery content evaporates makes the oil "separate" and come to the surface so you can

"fry off" the curry paste in it rather than having to add any other oil.
● The south and west of the country are shaped around the Gulf of Thailand, while the capital of Bangkok is crosshatched by canals emanating from the Chao Phraya River, so it's little wonder that fish and seafood form such a large part of the Thai diet. We used ling fillets for this recipe but you can use any boneless firm white fish fillet – blue eye, swordfish or sea perch are all good choices. Check for any small pieces of bone in the fillets and use tweezers to remove them. Salting your fingers

helps you get a better grip when pulling away the skin from the fillets. Don't add the fish until shortly before serving this curry: if overcooked, it can either disintegrate or toughen.
● You can buy fish stock in cartons from the supermarket, or canned or frozen from Asian food stores. Alternatively, you can make your own (page 117). Not only can you determine the final flavour this way, but you can make it in quantity and freeze the remainder in various-size containers to enable you to thaw the exact amount you want whenever you need it.

Chillies are sliced but usually not seeded before being used in a jungle curry

Rinse the brine from the pickled ka chai, then drain well before slicing it thinly

There is no need to separate the pickled green peppercorns from their stem before using them

pork jungle curry gaeng pak prik muu

PREPARATION TIME 20 MINUTES **COOKING TIME** 20 MINUTES

2 tablespoons peanut oil
¼ cup (75g) red curry paste (page 112)
750g pork fillet, sliced thinly
⅓ cup firmly packed fresh thai basil leaves
40g pickled ka chai, sliced thinly
150g thai eggplants, chopped coarsely
1 medium carrot (150g), sliced thinly
100g snake beans, chopped coarsely
227g can bamboo shoots, rinsed, drained
2 x 5cm stems pickled green peppercorns (10g)
2 fresh kaffir lime leaves, torn
1 litre (4 cups) vegetable stock (page 117)
4 fresh small red thai chillies, chopped coarsely

1 Place oil and curry paste in large saucepan; stir over heat until fragrant.
2 Add pork; cook, stirring, about 5 minutes or until browned all over.
3 Reserve about four large whole basil leaves for garnish. Add remaining basil leaves, ka chai, eggplant, carrot, beans, bamboo shoots, peppercorns, lime leaves and stock to pan; bring to a boil. Reduce heat; simmer, uncovered, about 10 minutes or until vegetables are tender. Stir in chilli.
4 Place curry in serving bowl; sprinkle with reserved thai basil leaves.

SERVES 4
per serving 18.2g fat; 1601kJ (382 cal)

TIPS

• There are two basic types of curry, one made with coconut milk and the other water- or stock-based. This popular meat curry falls into the latter category, being based on stock, and the resultant flavour is typically hot and spicy rather than sour.
• This fiery curry got its name from the originating cooks who, travelling through the jungle in Thailand's central plains, had to make do with what was available there. It has remained popular because it's easy to prepare and reminds the Thais of their links with the past.

• We used pickled thai green peppercorns, which are canned, still strung in clusters, but you can use an equivalent weight from a bottle of green peppercorns in brine. Without separating them from their strings, rinse and dry the peppercorns before using.
• The chillies most commonly used in Thai cooking are what we call birds-eye chillies (sometimes referred to as "scuds") and are especially fiery – if you want to decrease their heat, seed them before chopping. When doing so, always wear disposable kitchen gloves

because they can burn your skin. We found it better to decrease the number of chillies called for in a recipe than to seed the suggested quantity.
• Ka chai (can be spelled krachai or kah chi) is also known as lesser galangal, chinese ginger or finger-root. Similar to ginger in flavour with a slight hint of camphor, it is available from Asian supermarkets and greengrocers. The long, thin, brown fingerling-like roots are available fresh, dried, canned or pickled in brine; we used the last variation in this recipe.

Cut the fish fillets into fairly small pieces before processing into a paste

Roll heaped teaspoons of the processed fish mixture into small walnut-size balls

Reserve the coriander leaves, then finely chop the roots and stems together

fish ball and eggplant red curry   gaeng luk chin pla

PREPARATION TIME 20 MINUTES   **COOKING TIME** 15 MINUTES

500g firm white fish fillets, chopped coarsely

1 clove garlic, quartered

1 tablespoon finely chopped coriander root and stem mixture

1 tablespoon soy sauce

1 tablespoon cornflour

2 teaspoons peanut oil

2 tablespoons red curry paste (page 112)

400ml can coconut milk

½ cup (60g) pea eggplants

2 teaspoons grated palm sugar

1 tablespoon lime juice

1 tablespoon fish sauce

2 green onions, sliced thinly

½ cup (40g) bean sprouts

2 fresh long red thai chillies, sliced thinly

¼ cup loosely packed fresh coriander leaves

1 Blend or process fish with garlic, coriander mixture, soy sauce and cornflour until mixture forms a smooth paste; roll heaped teaspoons of mixture into balls.

2 Place oil and curry paste in large saucepan; stir over heat until fragrant. Add coconut milk; bring to a boil, stirring, until blended. Add fish balls and eggplants, reduce heat; simmer, uncovered, about 5 minutes or until fish balls are cooked through. Stir in sugar, juice, fish sauce and onion; stir until sugar dissolves.

3 Place curry in serving bowl; sprinkle with sprouts, chilli and coriander leaves.

SERVES 4
per serving   25.9g fat; 1621kJ (387 cal)

TIPS

● We used ling fillets here but you can use any firm white fish – bream, sea perch, swordfish or whiting, for example. Before chopping the fish fillets, check over the fish and remove any bones or skin: salting your fingers will help give you a better grip when pulling away skin, and you can use tweezers to pick out bones.

● Process the mixture earlier in the day and refrigerate the uncooked fish balls, covered, in a single layer on a tray, until shortly before you want to make the curry. The fish balls will firm and the flavours of the mixture meld during this time. You can also freeze the uncooked fish balls in snap-lock plastic bags.

● Both the stems and roots of coriander are used in Thai cooking so be certain to buy a bunch of fresh coriander with its roots intact. Wash the coriander under cold water, removing any dirt clinging to the roots. Reserve the leaves for garnish.

● Pea eggplants, makeua puong, are sold, fresh, in bunches like grapes or pickled in jars. They are more bitter than the slightly larger thai eggplants, which can be substituted in this recipe; both can be found in Asian grocery stores.

Press the air out of the plastic bag before freezing the kaffir lime leaves

Pound the palm sugar, using a mortar and pestle, until it becomes a fine powder

Roast the chopped peanuts in an ungreased heavy-base frying pan, stirring constantly

chicken panang curry gaeng panaeng gai

PREPARATION TIME 15 MINUTES **COOKING TIME** 20 MINUTES

2 x 400ml cans coconut milk
3 tablespoons panang curry paste (page 113)
2 tablespoons grated palm sugar
2 tablespoons fish sauce
2 fresh kaffir lime leaves, torn
2 tablespoons peanut oil
1kg chicken thigh fillets, quartered
100g snake beans, chopped coarsely
½ cup firmly packed fresh thai basil leaves
½ cup (75g) coarsely chopped roasted
  unsalted peanuts
2 fresh long red thai chillies, sliced thinly

1 Place coconut milk, paste, sugar, sauce and lime leaves in wok or large frying pan; bring to a boil. Reduce heat; simmer, stirring, about 15 minutes or until curry sauce mixture reduces by about a third.

2 Meanwhile, heat peanut oil in large frying pan; cook chicken, in batches, until browned lightly. Drain on absorbent paper.

3 Add beans, chicken and half of the basil leaves to curry sauce mixture; cook, uncovered, stirring occasionally, about 5 minutes or until beans are just tender and chicken is cooked through.

4 Place curry in serving bowl; sprinkle with peanuts, chilli and remaining basil.

SERVES 4
per serving 82.1g fat; 4347kJ (1038 cal)

TIPS

● Panang is a red Malaysian-style curry, made distinctive by its slightly sweet taste. Full and rich in flavour but low on chilli heat, this is a good curry to serve to people by way of an introduction to Thai food.
● Fish sauce is sometimes labelled by its Thai name, naam pla, or the Vietnamese name, nuoc naam: all varieties are almost identical. This sauce is salty and fairly potent, so use according to your

taste. Stir in half of the quantity called for in this recipe, taste the curry, then add the rest if you think the sauce needs any more.
● Thai basil, or horapa, is different from holy basil and sweet basil in both look and taste. Having smaller leaves and purplish stems, it has a slight liquorice or aniseed taste, and is one of the basic flavours that typify Thai cuisine.

● Kaffir lime leaves can be frozen: freeze in an airtight plastic bag and take what you need for each recipe.
● Palm sugar, from the coconut palm, is used throughout Asia, and its inclusion is responsible for the identifying sweetness of a panang curry. Also called jaggery, jawa or gula melaka, it is light brown to black in colour and usually sold in rock-hard cakes. If it is unavailable, you can substitute brown sugar.

Trim the piece of beef of any excess fat, then cut it into even-size 3cm pieces

Use the flat side of a heavy knife to bruise the cardamom pods and release their seeds

Discard the cardamom pods and star anise but reserve the spiced beef sauce

beef massaman curry gaeng masaman nuah

PREPARATION TIME 20 MINUTES **COOKING TIME** 2 HOURS

1kg beef skirt steak, cut into 3cm pieces

2 x 400ml cans coconut milk

1½ cups (375ml) beef stock (page 117)

5 cardamom pods, bruised

¼ teaspoon ground clove

2 star anise

1 tablespoon grated palm sugar

2 tablespoons fish sauce

1 tablespoon tamarind concentrate

2 tablespoons massaman curry paste (page 112)

2 teaspoons tamarind concentrate, extra

½ cup (125ml) beef stock, extra

8 baby brown onions (300g), halved

1 medium kumara (400g), chopped coarsely

¼ cup (35g) coarsely chopped unsalted roasted peanuts

2 green onions, sliced thinly

1 Place beef, half of the coconut milk, stock, cardamom, clove, star anise, sugar, sauce and tamarind in large saucepan; bring to a boil. Reduce heat; simmer, uncovered, about 1 hour 30 minutes or until beef is almost tender.

2 Strain beef over large bowl; reserve spicy beef sauce, discard cardamom and star anise.

3 Place curry paste in same cleaned pan; stir over heat until fragrant. Add remaining coconut milk, extra tamarind and stock; bring to a boil, stir for about 1 minute or until mixture is smooth. Add beef, brown onion, kumara and 1 cup of reserved spicy beef sauce; cook, uncovered, about 30 minutes or until vegetables and beef are tender.

4 Place curry in serving bowl; sprinkle with peanuts and green onion.

SERVES 4
per serving 54.6g fat; 3688kJ (881 cal)

TIPS

● Using spices carried to Thailand by Muslim traders from the West, this richly flavoured curry is redolent of the smell and taste of many Middle-Eastern dishes. It is one of the staples found on dining tables in the Muslim communities located mainly in the south of Thailand close to the Malaysian border.
● Skirt steak is made tooth-tender by long, slow cooking which also brings out the meat's depth of flavour. However, if time is a consideration, you can use beef rump in this recipe instead and cut the cooking time down in step 1 to about 30 minutes.
● Roast the peanuts in an ungreased heavy-base frying pan over medium heat, stirring constantly, until they are golden brown and just fragrant. Remove nuts from the hot pan immediately to prevent them from scorching. You'll find it easier to roast small amounts (½ cup or less) this way rather than in the oven.
● Cardamom pods act like packaging for the tiny brown seeds inside, keeping them fresh until required. You "bruise" a cardamom pod with the side of a heavy knife, crushing the husk and exposing the seeds; there is no need to separate the seeds and pod before using.

Use a heavy cleaver to chop the duck into 12 pieces that are all similar in size

Scrape the underside of the strainer with a spoon to retain as much of the thick tamarind pulp as possible

Stack the slices of ginger, then, using a sharp knife, cut through the stack to make long thin slivers

tamarind duck stir-fry   pad pet yang

PREPARATION TIME 20 MINUTES (PLUS STANDING TIME)   **COOKING TIME** 10 MINUTES

25g tamarind pulp
½ cup (125ml) boiling water
30g piece fresh ginger
1 tablespoon peanut oil
2 cloves garlic, crushed
2 fresh long red thai chillies, chopped finely
1 large whole barbecued duck (1kg),
    cut into 12 pieces
1 medium red capsicum (200g), sliced thinly
¼ cup (60ml) chicken stock (page 117)
2 tablespoons oyster sauce
1 tablespoon fish sauce
2 tablespoons grated palm sugar
200g baby bok choy, chopped coarsely
100g snow peas, sliced thinly
8 green onions, cut into 5cm lengths
⅓ cup firmly packed fresh coriander leaves

1 Soak tamarind pulp in the water for 30 minutes. Pour tamarind into a fine strainer over a small bowl; push as much pulp through the strainer as possible, scraping underside of strainer occasionally. Discard any tamarind solids left in strainer; reserve pulp liquid in bowl.

2 Slice peeled ginger thinly; stack slices, then slice again into thin slivers.

3 Heat oil in wok; stir-fry ginger, garlic and chilli until fragrant. Add duck and capsicum; stir-fry until capsicum is tender and duck is heated through.

4 Add stock, sauces, sugar and reserved pulp liquid, bring to a boil; boil, 1 minute. Add bok choy; stir-fry until just wilted. Add snow peas and onion; stir-fry until both are just tender. Remove from heat; toss coriander leaves through stir-fry.

SERVES 4
per serving 42.3g fat; 2381kJ (569 cal)

TIPS

● Tamarind is an important ingredient in Thai cooking, used mainly as a souring agent in marinades, pastes and sauces. Part of the pressed dried block is reconstituted by first being soaked in boiling water then strained through a fine sieve.
● Baby bok choy is sometimes called shanghai bok choy, chinese chard or white cabbage (pak kat farang); its mildly acrid, distinctively appealing taste has brought baby bok choy to the forefront of commonly used Asian greens.
● You can roast a whole raw duck if you wish, but it's simpler to purchase a large barbecued duck from your local Asian barbecued meat shop. Another alternative is to buy 750g of raw duck breast fillets (about 5 fillets); chop them coarsely and stir-fry until browned before adding with the capsicum.
● You can use either a Chinese-style heavy cleaver or kitchen scissors to separate the duck pieces. While the shop that sells you the duck can also chop it for you, we prefer to do it ourselves to control the size of the pieces and to ensure that any splinters of bone are discovered and discarded.

Slice only the subtle, sweet white bulb section of the spring onion for this recipe

Soak the noodles in a strainer that fits neatly into the bowl of water to make draining easier

Use two forks, tearing in opposite directions, to shred the cooked and drained silverside

crisp hot and sweet beef with noodles
pad ped wan nuah

PREPARATION TIME 20 MINUTES (PLUS STANDING TIME)   **COOKING TIME** 1 HOUR 45 MINUTES

750g piece corned silverside (beef)
1kg fresh wide rice noodles
¼ cup (60ml) peanut oil
3 cloves garlic, crushed
3 fresh small red thai chillies, sliced thinly
4 spring onions, sliced thinly
2 tablespoons fish sauce
¼ cup (65g) grated palm sugar
1 cup firmly packed fresh coriander leaves

1 Place beef, in packaging, in large saucepan, cover with cold water; bring to a boil, uncovered. Reduce heat; simmer, covered, 1 hour 30 minutes. Remove from pan, discard packaging; drain beef on rack over tray for 15 minutes.

2 Meanwhile, place noodles in large heatproof bowl; cover with boiling water, separate with fork, drain.

3 Trim excess fat from beef; using two forks, shred beef finely. Heat oil in wok; stir-fry beef, in batches, until browned all over and crisp. Drain on absorbent paper.

4 Stir-fry garlic, chilli and onion in same wok until onion softens. Add sauce and sugar; stir-fry until sugar dissolves. Return beef to wok with noodles; stir-fry gently until heated through. Remove from heat; toss coriander leaves through stir-fry.

SERVES 4
per serving 20.6g fat; 2589kJ (618 cal)

TIPS

● Corned silverside is best cooked in the cryovac packaging it is sold in; however, if you prefer, you can discard the packaging and simmer the meat submerged in water flavoured with some garlic and chillies, a few kaffir lime leaves and a stick of lemon grass. Allow the meat to cool slightly in the cooking liquid, then drain and shred it roughly while it is still warm.

● The fresh rice noodles used in this recipe can be found under various names – ho fun, sen yau, pho or kway tiau, depending on the nationality of the manufacturer. They can be purchased in various widths or, more commonly, in tea-towel-size sheets weighing about 500g each that you can cut into the width you prefer.

● Spring onions have larger bulbs than do green onions but have the same long green tops. If not using immediately, discard the top third of these green stems, then cut off the root end of the onion, pulling back and removing the attached skin-like layer. Wrap onions in absorbent paper, then place in an airtight plastic bag until ready to use.

Remove and discard the head and beak of each octopus before cleaning under cold water

Trim the root end from the green onions, then cut them into equal-size lengths

Discard the stems but keep the leaves whole when measuring the required amount of basil

stir-fried octopus with thai basil
pad pla muk horapa

PREPARATION TIME 20 MINUTES **COOKING TIME** 10 MINUTES

1kg baby octopus
2 teaspoons peanut oil
2 teaspoons sesame oil
2 cloves garlic, crushed
2 fresh small red thai chillies, sliced thinly
2 large red capsicums (500g), sliced thinly
6 green onions, cut into 2cm lengths
¼ cup firmly packed fresh thai basil leaves
¼ cup (60ml) fish sauce
¼ cup (65g) grated palm sugar
1 tablespoon kecap manis

1 Remove and discard the head and beak of each octopus; cut each octopus in half. Rinse under cold water; drain.

2 Heat peanut oil in wok; stir-fry octopus, in batches, until browned all over and tender. Cover to keep warm.

3 Heat sesame oil in same wok; stir-fry garlic, chilli and capsicum until capsicum is just tender. Return octopus to wok with remaining ingredients; stir-fry until basil leaves wilt and sugar dissolves.

SERVES 4
per serving 6.4g fat; 1048kJ (250 cal)

TIPS

● Thai basil, or horapa, is different from holy basil and sweet basil in both look and taste. Having smaller leaves and purplish stems, it has a slight liquorice or aniseed taste, and is one of the basic flavours that typify Thai cuisine.

● Be certain to have the wok and the oil preheated to very hot before adding the octopus so that it sears immediately instead of stewing. Octopus should be brown and very crisp rather than soft before removing from wok.

● Sieu wan is the Thai term for the dark, thick, sweet soy sauce usually called by its more familiar Indonesian and Malaysian name, kecap manis, which is also spelled ketjap manis.

As they are to be processed, there's no need to chop the chilli finely or crush the garlic

Peel the thai shallots and pull away the tissue-like outer layer of skin before slicing them

After trimming and quartering the unpeeled baby eggplants, cut each piece into 5cm lengths

pork with eggplant pad muu makeua

PREPARATION TIME 20 MINUTES **COOKING TIME** 25 MINUTES

3 fresh small red thai chillies, halved
6 cloves garlic, quartered
1 medium brown onion (150g),
    chopped coarsely
500g baby eggplants
2 tablespoons peanut oil
500g pork mince
1 tablespoon fish sauce
1 tablespoon soy sauce
1 tablespoon grated palm sugar
4 purple thai shallots, sliced thinly
150g snake beans, cut into 5cm lengths
1 cup loosely packed fresh thai basil leaves

1 Blend or process (or crush using mortar and pestle) chilli, garlic and onion until mixture forms a paste.

2 Quarter eggplants lengthways; slice each piece into 5cm lengths. Cook eggplant in large saucepan of boiling water until just tender; drain, pat dry with absorbent paper.

3 Heat oil in wok; stir-fry eggplant, in batches, until lightly browned. Drain on absorbent paper.

4 Stir-fry garlic paste in wok about 5 minutes or until lightly browned. Add pork; stir-fry until pork is changed in colour and cooked through. Add sauces and sugar; stir-fry until sugar dissolves. Add shallot and beans; stir-fry until beans are just tender. Return eggplant to wok; stir-fry, tossing gently until combined. Remove from heat; toss thai basil leaves through stir-fry.

SERVES 4
per serving 18.9g fat; 1387kJ (331 cal)

TIPS

● This pork and eggplant stir-fry, made simple by the addition of whole thai basil leaves and a chilli, onion and garlic paste, is an unusual and delicious way to cook eggplant. Ordinary eggplants in Thailand are long and green unlike the purple baby eggplants used here but, cooked, the taste is virtually the same.
● There's no need to disgorge (salt and drain) the eggplants in this recipe as

the very little bitter liquid they contain leaches out when they are boiled.
● Since the red chillies, garlic and brown onion are to be processed, blended or pounded using a mortar and pestle into a paste that, once fried, becomes the flavour essence of this stir-fry, there is no need to chop them extremely finely.

● Purple thai shallots (homm) are also called asian or pink shallots; used throughout South-East Asia, they are a member of the onion family but resemble garlic in that they grow in multiple-clove bulbs and are intensely flavoured. They are eaten fresh or deep-fried as a condiment as well as used pounded in curry pastes or tossed through stir-fries.

Use your mortar and pestle to crush the garlic, peppercorns, coriander seeds and root mixture into a paste	Fried shallot and fried garlic are available in Asian supermarkets canned or in cellophane bags	Chop about a tablespoon of coriander leaves coarsely but leave a similar amount whole

prawns with garlic goong kratiem

PREPARATION TIME 20 MINUTES (PLUS MARINATING TIME) **COOKING TIME** 5 MINUTES

1kg medium uncooked prawns
2 teaspoons coarsely chopped fresh coriander
  root and stem mixture
2 teaspoons dried coriander seeds
1 teaspoon dried green peppercorns
4 cloves garlic, quartered
2 tablespoons peanut oil
1 cup (80g) bean sprouts
1 tablespoon finely chopped fresh coriander
1 tablespoon packaged fried shallot
1 tablespoon packaged fried garlic
1 tablespoon fresh coriander leaves

1 Shell and devein prawns, leaving tails intact.

2 Crush coriander mixture, coriander seeds, peppercorns and garlic to a paste using mortar and pestle. Place paste in large bowl with prawns and half the oil; toss to coat prawns in marinade. Cover; refrigerate 3 hours or overnight.

3 Heat remaining oil in wok; stir-fry prawn mixture, in batches, until prawns are changed in colour. Remove from heat; toss bean sprouts and chopped coriander through stir-fry; serve sprinkled with fried shallot, fried garlic and coriander leaves.

SERVES 4
per serving 11.2g fat; 900kJ (215 cal)

TIPS

● The true Thai version of "garlic prawns" is cooked and eaten shells and all! While we have shelled and deveined the prawns in this recipe, you might try cooking them the way they do in Bangkok: the crisp shells are supposed to be loaded with calcium. This dish is also traditionally made with white peppercorns but we like the sweetness of the green variety.

● Some of the stems and roots of coriander are used in this recipe so buy a bunch of fresh coriander with its roots intact. Wash the coriander under cold water, removing any dirt clinging to the roots. Chop coriander roots and stems together to obtain the amount specified. Freeze the remainder of the chopped root and stem mixture, in teaspoon-size plastic-wrap parcels, for future use.

● Fried shallot (homm jiew) and garlic (kratiem jiew) are used as condiments on the table or sprinkled over cooked dishes. Both can be purchased canned or in cellophane bags at Asian grocery stores; once opened, leftovers will keep for months if tightly sealed. Make your own by slicing shallots or garlic thinly and shallow-frying in vegetable oil until golden-brown and crisp.

Stack lime leaves, then roll into a cigar shape before slicing thinly

Slice the unseeded chillies thinly; protect your skin by wearing disposable kitchen gloves

Remove the thai basil leaves from their stems before loosely packing in a measuring cup

chicken and thai basil stir-fry pad gai horapa

PREPARATION TIME 20 MINUTES **COOKING TIME** 15 MINUTES

2 tablespoons peanut oil
600g chicken breast fillets, sliced thinly
2 cloves garlic, crushed
1 teaspoon grated fresh ginger
4 fresh small red thai chillies, sliced thinly
4 kaffir lime leaves, shredded
1 medium brown onion (150g), sliced thinly
100g mushrooms, quartered
1 large carrot (180g), sliced thinly
¼ cup (60ml) oyster sauce
1 tablespoon soy sauce
1 tablespoon fish sauce
⅓ cup (80ml) chicken stock (page 117)
1 cup (80g) bean sprouts
¾ cup loosely packed fresh thai basil leaves

1 Heat half of the oil in wok; stir-fry chicken, in batches, until browned all over and cooked through.
2 Heat remaining oil in wok; stir-fry garlic, ginger, chilli, lime leaves and onion until onion softens and mixture is fragrant. Add mushroom and carrot; stir-fry until carrot is just tender. Return chicken to wok with sauces and stock; stir-fry until sauce thickens slightly. Remove from heat; toss bean sprouts and basil leaves through stir-fry.

SERVES 4
per serving 18.2g fat; 1449kJ (346 cal)

TIPS

● Any small red chillies can be used in place of the thai chillies (sometimes referred to as "scuds" because of their high heat) – and if you want to lessen their fire, remove the seeds. Wear disposable kitchen gloves while doing so because the seeds and membranes of these chillies can burn your skin.
● Fish sauce is sometimes called nuoc

naam on the label if it has a Vietnamese manufacturer; the Thai version, naam pla, is virtually identical.
● Thai basil, or horapa, is different from holy basil and sweet basil in both look and taste. Having smaller leaves and purplish stems, it has a slight liquorice or aniseed taste, and is one of the basic flavours that typify Thai cuisine.

● Fresh kaffir lime leaves are readily available in most greengrocers and many supermarkets. However, at a pinch, you can just as easily use fresh washed lemon or lime tree leaves or finely grated lime rind instead of the kaffir lime leaves (substitute each kaffir lime leaf with ½ teaspoon of finely grated lime rind).

Shell, devein, then remove the tails from the prawns before cutting them in half and processing them

Wear disposable kitchen gloves when seeding the chillies to avoid burning your fingers

After measuring the different breadcrumbs, combine them for use in coating prawn balls

deep-fried prawn balls tod mun goong

PREPARATION TIME 25 MINUTES (PLUS STANDING TIME) **COOKING TIME** 10 MINUTES

1kg large cooked king prawns
5 green onions, chopped finely
2 cloves garlic, crushed
4 fresh small red thai chillies, seeded,
  chopped finely
1 teaspoon grated fresh ginger
1 tablespoon cornflour
2 teaspoons fish sauce
¼ cup coarsely chopped fresh coriander
¼ cup (25g) packaged breadcrumbs
½ cup (35g) stale breadcrumbs
vegetable oil, for deep-frying
⅓ cup (80ml) sweet chilli sauce

1 Shell and devein prawns; cut in half. Blend or process prawn halves, pulsing, until chopped coarsely. Place in large bowl with onion, garlic, chilli, ginger, cornflour, sauce and coriander; mix well.

2 Using hands, roll rounded tablespoons of prawn mixture into balls. Roll prawn balls in combined breadcrumbs; place, in single layer, on plastic-wrap-lined tray. Cover, refrigerate 30 minutes.

3 Heat oil in wok or large saucepan; deep-fry prawn balls, in batches, until lightly browned and cooked through. Serve with sweet chilli sauce.

SERVES 4
per serving 10.8g fat; 1191kJ (284 cal)

TIPS

- Prawn balls are also good served with cucumber dipping sauce (page 4).
- Dip your fingers in cold water when shaping the prawn balls to prevent the mixture from sticking to them. Placing the uncooked prawn balls on a tray lined with plastic wrap and refrigerating them for at least half an hour will firm them and help ensure they don't fall apart during cooking.
- Uncooked prawn balls can be shaped a day ahead and kept, covered, overnight in the refrigerator.

- Make certain the oil is hot before you start frying the prawn balls, and try not to crowd them in the pan or they will cook unevenly. Turn them once, then keep the finished prawn balls warm by placing them on a tray lined with absorbent paper in a very slow oven while you finish frying the remainder.
- Keep the oil used for deep-frying for another time. After it has cooled completely, strain the oil through an absorbent-paper-lined sieve into a glass jar with a tight-fitting lid. Seal and

store in the refrigerator until required. Depending on what has been deep-fried in the oil, it's possible to re-use it, for deep-frying only, as many as three or four more times; when it starts to cloud or darken, discard it with other waste – not down the kitchen-sink drain.
- Uncooked prawn balls can also be threaded on skewers, sprayed lightly with cooking oil and char-grilled on the flat plate of a barbecue until slightly crisp. Take care not to overcook them as they will become tough and dry.

Score squid hood using the tip of a sharp knife before cutting it into 3cm pieces

Separate and discard the head and beak of each octopus; clean body under cold water

Only crisp a few thai basil leaves in each batch to avoid overcrowding and cooling the oil

mixed seafood with crisp thai basil
pad taleh horapa

PREPARATION TIME 25 MINUTES **COOKING TIME** 10 MINUTES

250g squid hoods
250g firm white fish fillets
12 medium uncooked king prawns (600g)
250g baby octopus
2 tablespoons peanut oil
1 clove garlic, crushed
2 fresh small red thai chillies, sliced thinly
1 medium carrot (120g), halved, sliced thinly
1 medium red capsicum (200g), sliced thinly
4 green onions, sliced thinly
1 tablespoon fish sauce
1 teaspoon oyster sauce
1 tablespoon lime juice
¼ cup (60ml) peanut oil, extra
⅓ cup loosely packed fresh thai basil leaves

1 Score squid in a diagonal pattern. Cut squid and fish into 3cm pieces; shell and devein prawns, leaving tails intact. Remove and discard the head and beak of each octopus; cut each octopus in half. Rinse under cold water; drain.

2 Heat half of the oil in wok or large saucepan; stir-fry seafood, in batches, until prawns are changed in colour, fish is cooked as desired, and squid and octopus are tender. Cover to keep warm.

3 Heat remaining oil in same wok; stir-fry garlic, chilli and carrot until carrot is just tender. Add capsicum; stir-fry until capsicum is just tender. Return seafood to wok with onion, sauces and juice; stir-fry, tossing gently, until hot.

4 Heat extra peanut oil in small frying pan until sizzling; fry basil leaves, in batches, until crisp but still green. Drain on absorbent paper. Top seafood with basil leaves.

SERVES 4
per serving 16.3g fat; 1455kJ (348 cal)

TIPS

● We used blue-eye for this recipe but you can use any boneless firm white fish fillet – ling, swordfish or sea perch are all good choices.
● Check for any small pieces of bone in the fish fillets and use tweezers to remove them. Salting your fingers helps you get a better grip when pulling away any remaining skin from the fish.

● Be certain to have the wok and the oil hot before adding the seafood so that it cooks immediately instead of stewing and thus toughening.
● Thai basil, or horapa, is different from holy basil and sweet basil in both look and taste. Having smaller leaves and purplish stems, it has a slight liquorice or aniseed taste, and is one of the basic flavours that typify Thai cuisine.

● The basil leaves should be completely dry before being fried or they will lower the temperature of the oil and become soggy rather than crisp. Work quickly with just a few at a time and bring the oil temperature back to sizzling between batches. Leaves are ready when the edges begin to curl slightly.
● Be careful of spitting oil when frying the basil leaves.

After scrubbing, use a small paring knife to clean any barnacles from the mussels

Use your fingers to pull the beard away from each of the tightly closed mussels

Any mussels that don't open during steaming time should be removed and discarded

mussels with basil and lemon grass   hoy op

PREPARATION TIME 20 MINUTES   **COOKING TIME** 10 MINUTES

1kg large mussels (approximately 30)
1 tablespoon peanut oil
1 medium brown onion (150g), chopped finely
2 cloves garlic, crushed
2 tablespoons thinly sliced fresh lemon grass
1 fresh small red thai chilli, chopped finely
1 cup (250ml) dry white wine
2 tablespoons lime juice
2 tablespoons fish sauce
½ cup loosely packed fresh thai basil leaves
½ cup (125ml) coconut milk
1 fresh small red thai chilli, seeded, sliced thinly
2 green onions, sliced thinly

1 Scrub mussels under cold water; remove beards.
2 Heat oil in wok or large frying pan; stir-fry brown onion, garlic, lemon grass and chopped chilli until onion softens and mixture is fragrant.
3 Add wine, juice and sauce; bring to a boil. Add mussels; reduce heat, simmer, covered, about 5 minutes or until mussels open (discard any that do not).
4 Meanwhile, shred half of the basil finely. Add shredded basil and coconut milk to wok; stir-fry until heated through. Place mussel mixture in serving bowl; sprinkle with sliced chilli, green onion and remaining basil.

SERVES 4
per serving 12.2g fat; 877kJ (209 cal)

TIPS

● Rich coconut flavour and just the right amount of spice make this classic the favourite it is, both in Thailand and in Thai restaurants around the world.
● You can use whichever mussel type is available at the fish markets on the day for this recipe; calculate on about four per serving, regardless of weight. Always buy the mussel variety that is in season.

● Keeping mussels wrapped tightly and weighted down, in the refrigerator, helps prevent them opening and maintains their quality.
● When mussels are roasted or steamed, they only taste of mussel; however, when steamed in an appetising mixture such as seen here, mussels take on its aromatic qualities, which improves the flavour of the mussels.

● Coconut milk should be refrigerated after using the single cup called for here; it will keep up to a week. We do not suggest that you freeze leftover coconut milk because it increases the likelihood of curdling when the thawed milk is used in cooking. We also suggest that you avoid buying cans of sweetened coconut milk – it is not recommended for Thai cooking.

Scoring the fish allows the herbs, lime and chilli flavours to permeate the flesh

Position two pieces of lemon grass diagonally across the centre of the banana leaf piece

Top fish with herb mixture, then fold opposite corners of leaf and enclose parcel using cotton string

hot and sour fish steamed in banana leaves
hor neung mok pla

PREPARATION TIME 25 MINUTES (PLUS MARINATING TIME)   **COOKING TIME** 20 MINUTES

4 medium whole bream (1.8kg)

1 large banana leaf

4 fresh small red thai chillies, seeded, sliced thinly

2 fresh kaffir lime leaves, shredded finely

2 green onions, sliced thinly

¼ cup loosely packed fresh coriander leaves

¼ cup loosely packed fresh thai basil leaves

2 sticks fresh lemon grass

cotton string

LIME AND SWEET CHILLI DRESSING

¼ cup (60ml) sweet chilli sauce

2 tablespoons fish sauce

2 tablespoons lime juice

2 tablespoons peanut oil

1 clove garlic, crushed

1 teaspoon grated fresh ginger

TIPS

● If bream is unavailable, use any of your favourite whole firm-fleshed fish for this recipe. Cooking times will vary depending on the fish you select.
● Steaming is best done in a bamboo steamer because, in a metal one, condensation on the lid can drip on to the food and spoil the appearance. If you have to use a metal steamer, cover the fish with absorbent paper that doesn't touch the steamer.
● Fish parcels can also be cooked on a heated grill plate or barbecue for about 15 minutes or until the fish is cooked as desired.

1 Make lime and sweet chilli dressing.

2 Score fish both sides through thickest part of flesh; place on large tray, drizzle with half of the lime and sweet chilli dressing. Cover; refrigerate 1 hour.

3 Meanwhile, trim banana leaf into four 30cm squares. Using tongs, dip one square at a time into large saucepan of boiling water; remove immediately. Rinse under cold water; pat dry with absorbent paper.

4 Place leaves on work surface. Combine chilli, lime leaves, onion, coriander and basil in medium bowl. Halve lemon grass sticks lengthways, then halve crossways; you will have eight pieces.

5 Place two pieces cut lemon grass on each leaf; place one fish on each. Top fish with equal amounts of the herb mixture then fold opposite corners of the leaf to enclose centre part of fish; secure each parcel with cotton string.

6 Place parcels, in single layer, in large bamboo steamer; steam, covered, in 2 batches, over wok or large frying pan of simmering water about 15 minutes or until fish is cooked through. Serve fish still in parcel, sprinkled with remaining dressing.

lime and sweet chilli dressing Combine ingredients in screw-top jar; shake well.

SERVES 4
per serving 22.1g fat; 1708kJ (408 cal)

Sea salt should be sprinkled uniformly over the fish cutlets before they are grilled

Roast the cashews in a large heavy-base frying pan, stirring, until the cashews are fragrant

Pour the hot dressing through a strainer into a heatproof bowl after the sugar has dissolved

salmon cutlets with green apple salad
yang pla yum poodza

PREPARATION TIME 20 MINUTES **COOKING TIME** 10 MINUTES (PLUS COOLING TIME)

½ teaspoon sea salt
4 salmon cutlets (680g)
2 medium apples (300g), sliced thinly
2 green onions, sliced thinly
1 medium red onion (170g), sliced thinly
1½ cups loosely packed fresh mint leaves
¾ cup loosely packed fresh coriander leaves
½ cup (125ml) lemon juice
¾ cup (110g) roasted unsalted cashews

PALM SUGAR DRESSING
⅓ cup (65g) grated palm sugar
2 tablespoons fish sauce
2 teaspoons grated fresh ginger

1 Sprinkle salt evenly over fish. Cook fish on heated oiled grill plate (or grill or barbecue) until browned both sides and cooked as desired.
2 Meanwhile, combine apple, onions, mint, coriander and juice in large bowl; pour over half of the palm sugar dressing, toss to combine. Divide fish among serving plates; top with salad, then cashews. Drizzle remaining dressing over fish.
   palm sugar dressing Combine ingredients in small saucepan; bring to a boil. Remove from heat; strain. Cool before using.

SERVES 4
per serving 24g fat; 2015kJ (481 cal)

TIPS

● In Thailand, this dish is made with jujubes (a fruit known as the "thai apple") but we have substituted green apples for ease in obtaining ingredients. Called poodza in Thailand, the jujube is a small, oval fruit, similar in taste and texture to an apple, which is eaten raw, juiced or dried. The fruit's thin edible skin changes from green to red as it ripens, which is when it is at its most sweet and crisp, and most reminiscent of an apple.

● If you don't want to contend with the bones and skin of a cutlet, you can also use fillets in this recipe. Cooking times will change slightly for each different kind and thickness of fish you select but salmon is at its best if slightly underdone, to keep texture moist.
● Stir the cashews constantly when roasting them in a frying pan or wok because they can burn and become unpalatable very quickly.

● While salmon's firm flesh makes it a good fish to grill, if the oiled grill plate is too cool when the salmon hits it, the fish will stick and stew rather than crisp. If it is too hot, the delicate flavour of the fish will be lost. Medium-high heat under the plate will help to ensure you get perfect results.
● Don't slice the apples until you're ready to toss with the dressing because the flesh will brown when exposed to air.

Wear kitchen gloves while grating the turmeric to avoid turning your fingers yellow

The galangal piece need only be halved because it is discarded before serving fish

Don't overcook the fish; also, take care when removing it from the sauce or it could fall apart

fish in spicy coconut cream   pla tom kati

PREPARATION TIME 15 MINUTES   **COOKING TIME** 20 MINUTES

2 teaspoons peanut oil
2 cloves garlic, crushed
1 teaspoon grated fresh ginger
20g piece fresh turmeric, grated finely
2 fresh small red thai chillies, sliced thinly
1½ cups (375ml) fish stock (page 117)
400ml can coconut cream
20g piece fresh galangal, halved
1 stick fresh lemon grass, cut into 2cm pieces
4 firm white fish fillets (800g)
2 tablespoons fish sauce
2 green onions, sliced thinly

1 Heat oil in wok or large frying pan; cook garlic, ginger, turmeric and chilli, stirring, until fragrant. Add stock, coconut cream, galangal and lemon grass; bring to a boil. Add fish, reduce heat; simmer, covered, about 8 minutes or until fish is cooked as desired. Remove and discard galangal and lemon grass pieces.

2 Using slotted spoon, remove fish carefully from sauce; place in serving bowl, cover to keep warm. Bring sauce to a boil; boil 5 minutes. Remove from heat; stir in fish sauce and onion. Pour sauce over fish in bowl.

SERVES 4
per serving 24.5g fat; 1735kJ (414 cal)

TIPS

● This recipe is a good example of a typical southern coastal Thai method of cooking local fish. Turmeric and coconut have a natural affinity with one another and with simple white fish, as can be seen in many similar Indonesian, Malaysian and Indian fish recipes.
● Coconut milk/cream is not the juice found inside a coconut, but the diluted liquid pressed from the white flesh of a mature coconut. After the liquid settles, the cream and the "milk" (thin white fluid) separate naturally. Coconut (kati) cream is obtained commercially by pressing grated coconut flesh alone, without the addition of water.
● Turmeric (kamin), a rhizome (a knob-like underground-growing stem) related to ginger, must be grated or pounded to release its somewhat acrid aroma and pungent flavour. Known for the golden colour it bestows on the dishes in which it's used, fresh turmeric can be substituted with the more common dried powder (use 2 teaspoons of ground turmeric plus 1 teaspoon of sugar for every 20g of fresh turmeric called for in a recipe).
● Galangal (ka) is another rhizome with a hot ginger-citrusy flavour. It is used similarly to ginger and garlic — fresh as an ingredient, or dried and ground as a seasoning.
● Peel and cut any remaining turmeric and galangal into 20g pieces, then wrap individually in plastic and freeze for future use. They'll keep for months and are easier to grate when frozen.

glutinous

jasmine

black

thai rices

Kin khao in Thai means both "rice" and "to eat": a meal without this staple food is simply unthinkable. Plain rice is served as the main part of every meal with various curries, soups and sauces presented in smaller bowls, their purpose being just to flavour the rice rather than being a main dish.

There are three main varieties grown in Thailand: jasmine white rice, sweet glutinous (sticky) rice and black (or purple) rice. Each of the following rice cooking methods makes enough rice for four servings.

glutinous

Thai glutinous rice (also known as "sweet" or "sticky" rice) is a uniquely flavoured rice that is eaten, formed into small balls, with the fingers and dipped into savoury dishes, to soak up their sauces. People in the north of Thailand eat glutinous rice as the main component of their diets. The grains are short, fat and chalky white in the centre, and cooked become soft and "sticky". **Note** Glutinous rice is a particular variety of rice that requires long soaking and steaming; other varieties of rice cannot be cooked by this method successfully.

PREPARATION TIME
10 MINUTES (PLUS SOAKING TIME)
COOKING TIME 40 MINUTES

2 cups (400g) glutinous rice

1 Rinse rice in strainer or colander under cold water until water runs clear. Soak rice in large bowl of cold water overnight.
2 Drain rice. Line metal or bamboo steamer with muslin; place rice in steamer, cover tightly. Place steamer over large saucepan of boiling water, taking care that the bottom of the steamer does not touch the boiling water. Steam rice, tightly covered, about 40 minutes or until cooked as desired. Do not remove lid or stir rice during cooking time.
SERVES 4
per serving 0.5g fat;
1470kJ (351 cal)

jasmine

Thai jasmine rice is recognised around the world as having a particular aromatic quality that can almost be described as perfumed or floral.
A long-grained white rice, it is sometimes used in place of the more-expensive basmati rice in South-East Asia. Jasmine rice is rather moist in texture and clings together after cooking; adding salt during cooking is not recommended because it destroys the delicate flavour of the rice. No Thai meal is complete without a large bowl of hot jasmine rice at its epicentre.

PREPARATION TIME
1 MINUTE (PLUS STANDING TIME)
COOKING TIME 12 MINUTES

2 cups (400g) jasmine rice
1 litre (4 cups) cold water

1 Combine rice and the water in large saucepan having a tight-fitting lid; bring to a boil, stirring occasionally.
2 Reduce heat as low as possible; cook rice, covered tightly, about 12 minutes or until all water is absorbed and rice is cooked as desired. Do not remove lid or stir rice during cooking time. Remove from heat; stand, covered, 10 minutes before serving.
SERVES 4
per serving 0.5g fat;
1470kJ (351 cal)

black

Black rice is also known as purple rice because, although a deep charcoal when raw, after cooking it turns a purplish-black colour. A medium-grain unmilled rice, with a white kernel under the black bran, it has a nutty, whole-grain flavour and is crunchy to the bite, similar to wild rice.

PREPARATION TIME
2 MINUTES
COOKING TIME 20 MINUTES

2 cups (400g) black rice

1 Rinse rice in strainer under cold water until water runs clear.
2 Place rice in large saucepan of boiling water; boil, uncovered, stirring occasionally, about 20 minutes or until rice is cooked as desired. Drain; stand, covered, 10 minutes before serving.
SERVES 4
per serving 0.6g fat;
842kJ (201 cal)

Soak the rice in a fine strainer placed in a large bowl of water to make draining easy

Add a healthy "pinch" of saffron threads directly into the rice mixture without soaking first

Fluff the cooked rice with a fork to ensure that the grains separate even though the mixture is creamy

yellow coconut rice   khao kamin

PREPARATION TIME 5 MINUTES (PLUS STANDING TIME) **COOKING TIME** 15 MINUTES

1¾ cups (350g) long-grain white rice
1¼ cups (310ml) water
400ml can coconut cream
½ teaspoon salt
1 teaspoon sugar
½ teaspoon ground turmeric
pinch saffron threads

1 Soak rice in large bowl of cold water for 30 minutes. Pour rice into strainer; rinse under cold water until water runs clear. Drain.

2 Place rice and remaining ingredients in large heavy-base saucepan; cover, bring to boil, stirring occasionally. Reduce heat; simmer, covered, about 15 minutes or until rice is tender. Remove from heat; stand, covered, 5 minutes.

SERVES 4
per serving 21.1g fat; 2167kJ (518 cal)

TIPS

● In the southern region of Thailand, plentiful coconut milk and fresh turmeric are frequently combined in various dishes. Neither as hot as a curry nor as wet as a soup, this rich, savoury rice dish's subtle flavour makes a good accompaniment to a meal's highly spiced dishes, helping temper their heat. The flavour of the coconut cream is important in this dish, and, if you can get fresh turmeric, grate enough to fill a level teaspoon and use it instead of the dried version.
● Saffron is available in strands or ground form. It imparts a yellow-orange colour to food once infused.

● Place the rice in a wire-mesh strainer or small-holed colander, then submerge it in a large saucepan or bowl filled with cold water. When soaking time has elapsed, simply lift out the strainer and allow the rice to drain. Rinse the rice in the same strainer or colander and again allow it to drain.
● Coconut milk/cream is not the juice found inside a coconut, but the diluted liquid pressed from the white meat of a mature coconut. Coconut (kati) cream is obtained commercially by pressing grated coconut flesh alone, without water, using specialised machinery.

● Do not stir rice at all while it is simmering. The length of time the rice needs to simmer to become tender will depend on temperature variations among stove-tops.
● This recipe is easy to cook in a microwave oven. Place ingredients in a large microwave-safe bowl; cover with absorbent paper and cook on HIGH (100%) for 10 minutes. Pause, stir; cook, covered with absorbent paper, a further 2 minutes on HIGH (100%). Pause and mix with a fork; cook uncovered on LOW (50%) for 2 minutes.

Spread the rice out in an even layer on a tray lined with baking paper and then refrigerate it

Green chillies can be called thai chillies but are sometimes sold as jalapeño or serrano chillies

Thai basil leaves should be added to the wok off the heat, just before you serve the rice

chicken and thai basil fried rice
khao pad gai horapa

PREPARATION TIME 15 MINUTES **COOKING TIME** 10 MINUTES

¼ cup (60ml) peanut oil
1 medium brown onion (150g), chopped finely
3 cloves garlic, crushed
2 fresh long green thai chillies, seeded, chopped finely
1 tablespoon brown sugar
500g chicken breast fillets, chopped coarsely
2 medium red capsicums (400g), sliced thinly
200g green beans, chopped coarsely
4 cups cooked jasmine rice
2 tablespoons fish sauce
2 tablespoons soy sauce
½ cup loosely packed fresh thai basil leaves

1 Heat oil in wok; stir-fry onion, garlic and chilli until onion softens. Add sugar; stir-fry until dissolved. Add chicken; stir-fry until lightly browned. Add capsicum and beans; stir-fry until vegetables are just tender and chicken is cooked through.

2 Add rice and sauces; stir-fry, tossing gently to combine. Remove from heat; add basil leaves, toss gently to combine.

SERVES 4
per serving 21.7g fat; 1922kJ (459 cal)

TIPS

● You need to cook about 2 cups of jasmine rice the day before you want to make this recipe.
● One of the secrets to making perfect fried rice is that the rice must be cold before using it. Make the rice far enough in advance so that it is chilled completely and quite dry, in order to prevent it sticking together in clumps when added to the wok. After cooking the rice, drain it if necessary, then spread in a single layer on a tray lined with baking paper or greaseproof paper. Cover with absorbent paper (condensation trapped below plastic wrap will keep the rice too wet) and refrigerate for at least 3 hours or overnight.
● Frozen rice is particularly good for frying: after it has partially thawed, break the rice apart and spread it on sheets of absorbent paper before you start cooking.
● Picking up about a quarter of the rice at a time, break it up with your fingers so the grains are already separate when they hit the wok.
● The second secret to perfect fried rice is that it must be stir-fried over as high a heat as possible in the briefest amount of time, so it is important that all ingredients are prepared and ready for use before you begin to heat your wok.
● Pouring the sauces down the hot side of the wok rather than directly into the centre brings them to sizzling point before they mix with the wok's contents.

Add the cooled rice to the wok in small amounts so it fries without clumping

Centre about a quarter of the fried rice and crab filling in the omelette just after it sets

Fold all four sides of omelette inwards until they meet and form a somewhat square "parcel"

crab fried rice in omelette   khai yud sai khao puu

PREPARATION TIME 15 MINUTES   **COOKING TIME** 25 MINUTES

¼ cup (60ml) peanut oil
4 green onions, chopped finely
2 fresh small red thai chillies, chopped finely
1 tablespoon red curry paste (page 112)
2 cups cooked jasmine rice
250g fresh crab meat
2 tablespoons lime juice
2 tablespoons fish sauce
8 eggs
2 tablespoons water
1 lime, cut into wedges

1 Heat 1 tablespoon of the oil in wok; stir-fry onion and chopped chilli until onion softens. Add curry paste; stir-fry until mixture is fragrant.

2 Add rice; stir-fry until heated through. Remove from heat; place in large bowl. Add crab meat, juice and sauce; toss to combine.

3 Whisk eggs with the water in medium bowl. Heat about a quarter of the remaining oil in same cleaned wok; pour a quarter of the egg mixture into wok. Cook, tilting pan, over low heat until almost set. Spoon a quarter of the fried rice into centre of the omelette; using spatula, fold four sides of omelette over to enclose filling.

4 Press omelette firmly with spatula; turn carefully to brown other side. Remove omelette from wok; cover to keep warm. Repeat process with remaining oil, egg mixture and fried rice. Place omelettes on serving plate; serve with lime.

SERVES 4
per serving 26.3g fat; 1599kJ (382 cal)

TIPS

● You need to cook ⅔ cup of jasmine rice the day before making this recipe.
● If you don't want to use crab, you can substitute 250g small shelled cooked prawns for it if you wish.
● If the red curry paste is too hot, you can substitute either yellow or panang curry paste (page 113) for it; both go very well with seafood.

● One of the secrets to making perfect fried rice is that the rice must be cold before using it. Make the rice far enough in advance so that it is chilled completely and quite dry, in order to prevent it sticking together in clumps when added to the wok. After cooking the rice, drain it if necessary, then spread in a single layer on a tray lined with baking paper

or greaseproof paper. Cover with absorbent paper (condensation trapped below plastic wrap will keep the rice too wet) and refrigerate for at least 3 hours or overnight.
● Frozen rice is particularly good for frying: after it has partially thawed, break the rice apart and spread it on sheets of absorbent paper just before you start cooking.

Deep-fry the noodles in very small batches to ensure that they crisp evenly without clumping

Combine cooled noodles and fried onions in bowl with green onions and coriander leaves

Separate remaining noodles with a fork while they're soaking in the boiling water

chiang mai noodles khao soi gai

PREPARATION TIME 20 MINUTES **COOKING TIME** 20 MINUTES

vegetable oil, for deep-frying
500g fresh egg noodles
1 large brown onion (200g), sliced thinly
2 green onions, sliced thinly
¼ cup loosely packed fresh coriander leaves
¼ cup (75g) red curry paste (page 112)
2 cloves garlic, crushed
¼ teaspoon ground turmeric
2 cups (500ml) water
400ml can coconut milk
500g chicken breast fillets, sliced thinly
¼ cup (60ml) fish sauce
1 tablespoon soy sauce
2 tablespoons grated palm sugar
2 teaspoons lime juice
2 tablespoons coarsely chopped fresh coriander
1 fresh long red thai chilli, seeded, sliced thinly

1 Heat oil in wok; deep-fry about 100g of the noodles, in batches, until crisp. Drain on absorbent paper.
2 Using same heated oil, deep-fry brown onion, in batches, until lightly browned and crisp. Drain on absorbent paper. Combine fried noodles, fried onion, green onion and coriander leaves in small bowl. Cool oil; remove from wok and reserve for another use.
3 Place remaining noodles in large heatproof bowl, cover with boiling water; use fork to separate noodles, drain.
4 Cook paste, garlic and turmeric in same cleaned wok, add the water and coconut milk; bring to a boil. Reduce heat; simmer, stirring, 2 minutes. Add chicken; cook, stirring, about 5 minutes or until chicken is cooked through. Add sauces, sugar and juice; cook, stirring, until sugar dissolves. Stir in chopped coriander.
5 Divide drained noodles among serving bowls; spoon chicken curry mixture into each bowl, then top with fried noodle mixture. Sprinkle chilli slices over each bowl.

SERVES 4
per serving 33.5g fat; 3358kJ (802 cal)

TIPS

• The favourite noodle dish of Thailand's north, khao soi is a combination of soft and crisp fresh rice or egg noodles in a meat or poultry curry sauce made rich with the addition of coconut milk – which makes it distinct from the noodle dishes of other regions.
• You can use any other type of noodle in this dish. Thin rice stick (sen lek) or fresh thin wheat noodles, such

as peking or shanghai, can be used instead of fresh egg noodles (ba mee). Each type of noodle requires different preparation so follow the instructions on the package.
• Keep the oil used for deep-frying for another time. After it has cooled completely, strain the oil through an absorbent-paper-lined sieve into a glass jar with a tight-fitting lid. Seal and

store in the refrigerator until required. Depending on what has been deep-fried in the oil, it's possible to re-use it, as a deep-frying medium only, as many as three or four more times; when it starts to cloud or darken, discard it with other waste – not down the kitchen-sink drain.
• The deep-fried noodles and onion can be fried a day ahead and stored in separate airtight containers.

After washing and drying the baby bok choy, cut them lengthways into quarters

Separate the delicate noodles gently with a fork while they're soaking to avoid tearing them

Take care when tossing the noodles in the wok that they do not get broken up or mashed

sweet soy fried noodles pad sieu

PREPARATION TIME 15 MINUTES **COOKING TIME** 15 MINUTES

1kg fresh wide rice noodles
2 teaspoons sesame oil
2 cloves garlic, crushed
2 fresh small red thai chillies, sliced thinly
600g chicken thigh fillets, chopped coarsely
250g baby bok choy, quartered lengthways
4 green onions, sliced thinly
2 tablespoons kecap manis
1 tablespoon oyster sauce
1 tablespoon fish sauce
1 tablespoon grated palm sugar
¼ cup coarsely chopped fresh coriander
1 tablespoon fried onion

1 Place noodles in large heatproof bowl; cover with boiling water, separate with fork, drain.
2 Heat oil in large wok; stir-fry garlic and chilli until fragrant. Add chicken; stir-fry until lightly browned. Add bok choy and green onion; stir-fry until green onion softens and chicken is cooked through.
3 Add noodles with kecap manis, sauces and sugar; stir-fry, tossing gently to combine. Remove from heat; add coriander, tossing gently to combine. Sprinkle with fried onion.

SERVES 4
per serving 14.6g fat; 2176kJ (520 cal)

TIPS

● This is another classic fried noodle dish that has become a Thai "fast food", eaten by people all over the country for lunch and as a snack.
● Sieu is the Thai thick sweet soy sauce usually sold by its Indonesian/Malaysian name, kecap manis. Depending on the brand, the soy's sweetness is derived from the addition of either molasses or palm sugar when it's made. While there is no real substitute, dissolving some brown sugar in soy sauce will suffice.

● The fresh rice noodles to use in this recipe can be found under various names – ho fun, sen yau, pho or kway tiau, depending on the nationality of the manufacturer. They can be purchased in various widths or, more commonly, in tea-towel-size sheets weighing about 500g each, which you cut into the width noodle you prefer. These noodles do not need pre-cooking but do require a hot-water "bath" in order to separate them into individual strands before draining and frying.

● Fried onion, sold in Asian grocery stores packed in jars or in cellophane bags, is used as a topping for various Thai rice and noodle dishes, and also served as a condiment as part of a Thai meal. Fried garlic is sold and used in the same way. Both can be made at home by cutting onions and garlic into paper-thin slices, then deep-frying them in peanut oil, in batches; drain the crisp pieces on absorbent paper before storing them in airtight containers.

Press the tamarind with the back of a spoon to extract as much liquid as possible

Cut preserved turnip into fairly small pieces to make it easier to crush when preparing the paste

Pound dried shrimp, preserved turnip, garlic and spices into a paste, using a mortar and pestle

thai fried rice stick noodles   pad thai

PREPARATION TIME 20 MINUTES (PLUS STANDING TIME) **COOKING TIME** 10 MINUTES

40g tamarind pulp
½ cup (125ml) boiling water
2 tablespoons grated palm sugar
⅓ cup (80ml) sweet chilli sauce
⅓ cup (80ml) fish sauce
375g rice stick noodles
12 medium uncooked prawns (500g)
2 cloves garlic, crushed
2 tablespoons finely chopped preserved turnip
2 tablespoons dried shrimp
1 tablespoon grated fresh ginger
2 fresh small red thai chillies, seeded, chopped coarsely
1 tablespoon peanut oil
250g pork mince
3 eggs, beaten lightly
2 cups (160g) bean sprouts
4 green onions, sliced thinly
⅓ cup coarsely chopped fresh coriander
¼ cup (35g) coarsely chopped roasted unsalted peanuts
1 lime, quartered

1 Soak tamarind pulp in the boiling water for 30 minutes. Pour tamarind into fine strainer over small bowl; push as much tamarind pulp through strainer as possible, scraping underside of strainer occasionally. Discard any tamarind solids left in strainer; reserve pulp liquid in bowl. Mix sugar and sauces into bowl with tamarind; reserve.

2 Meanwhile, place noodles in large heatproof bowl; cover with boiling water, stand until noodles just soften; drain.

3 Shell and devein prawns, leaving tails intact.

4 Blend or process (or crush using mortar and pestle) garlic, turnip, shrimp, ginger and chilli until mixture forms a paste.

5 Heat oil in wok; stir-fry spice paste until fragrant. Add pork; stir-fry until just cooked through. Add prawns; stir-fry 1 minute. Add egg; stir-fry until egg just sets. Add noodles, tamarind mixture, sprouts and half of the onion; stir-fry, tossing gently until combined. Remove from heat; toss remaining green onion, coriander and nuts through pad thai. Serve with lime wedges.

SERVES 4
per serving 19.7g fat; 2576kJ (615 cal)

TIPS

● Although pad thai is quick to cook, all the ingredients must be ready to use the minute you heat the wok. While the tamarind and noodles are soaking, use this time to prepare the remaining ingredients.
● Dried shrimp (goong hang) are salted sun-dried prawns ranging in size from not much larger than a rice seed to about 1cm in length. They are sold, shelled as a rule, in packages in all Asian grocery stores.
● Tamarind is an important ingredient in Thai cooking, used mainly as a souring agent in marinades, pastes and dressings. It is also used in the manufacture of many Thai ketchups and sauces.
● Preserved turnip (hua chai po or cu cai muoi on the label) is also called dried radish because it is very similar to dried daikon. Sold packaged whole or in slices, it is very salty and should be rinsed and dried well before being used in cooking. Preserved turnip is an essential ingredient for an authentic pad thai.

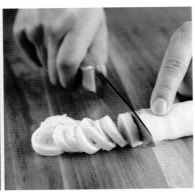

Deep-fry vermicelli in small batches as they burn easily and expand quickly

Swirl the wok as soon as the egg is added to make omelette evenly thin all over

Roll each omelette into a tight cigar shape before slicing it into wafer-thin wheels

crisp fried noodles mee krob

PREPARATION TIME 35 MINUTES **COOKING TIME** 20 MINUTES

150g fresh silken firm tofu
vegetable oil, for deep-frying
125g rice vermicelli
2 tablespoons peanut oil
2 eggs, beaten lightly
1 tablespoon water
2 cloves garlic, crushed
2 fresh small red thai chillies, chopped finely
1 fresh small green thai chilli, chopped finely
2 tablespoons grated palm sugar
2 tablespoons fish sauce
2 tablespoons tomato sauce
1 tablespoon rice wine vinegar
200g pork mince
200g small shelled cooked prawns,
   chopped coarsely
6 green onions, sliced thinly
¼ cup firmly packed fresh coriander leaves

TIPS

● Thais serve mee krob by dividing the vermicelli among bowls, then presenting the sauce in a separate bowl. Onion, omelette and coriander are also served in separate small bowls, with each diner taking as much as desired of the three to sprinkle over the top of his or her dish.
● Be careful when deep-frying the vermicelli: slide rather than drop them into the oil to help prevent splattering. Add them in small batches so the oil temperature doesn't reduce. Vermicelli puff immediately and must be removed from the oil quickly with a metal slotted spoon or tongs.

1 Pat tofu all over with absorbent paper; cut into slices, then cut each slice into 1cm-wide matchsticks. Spread tofu on tray lined with absorbent paper; cover tofu with more absorbent paper, stand at least 10 minutes.
2 Meanwhile, heat vegetable oil in wok or large saucepan; deep-fry vermicelli quickly, in batches, until puffed. Drain on absorbent paper.
3 Using same heated oil, deep-fry drained tofu, in batches, until lightly browned. Drain on absorbent paper. Cool oil; remove from wok and reserve for another use.
4 Heat 2 teaspoons of the peanut oil in same cleaned wok; add half of the combined egg and water, swirl wok to make thin omelette. Cook, uncovered, until egg is just set. Remove from wok; roll omelette, cut into thin strips. Heat 2 more teaspoons of the peanut oil in same wok; repeat process with remaining egg mixture.
5 Combine garlic, chillies, sugar, sauces and vinegar in small bowl; pour half of the chilli mixture into small jug, reserve.
6 Combine pork in bowl with remaining half of the chilli mixture. Heat remaining peanut oil in same wok; stir-fry pork mixture about 5 minutes or until pork is cooked through. Add prawns; stir-fry 1 minute. Add tofu; stir-fry, tossing gently to combine.
7 Remove wok from heat; add reserved chilli mixture and half of the onion, toss to combine. Add vermicelli; toss gently to combine. Remove from heat; sprinkle with remaining onion, omelette strips and coriander leaves.

SERVES 4
per serving 23.2g fat; 2015kJ (481 cal)

Chop the tofu into the finest possible dice before draining it on a paper-lined tray

Since it is not cooked in the larb, the lemon grass must be chopped as finely as possible

Deep-fry the chopped tofu in very small batches until it is crisp and just golden brown

larb tofu   larb tao hu

PREPARATION TIME 20 MINUTES (PLUS STANDING TIME) **COOKING TIME** 10 MINUTES

900g fresh firm silken tofu
peanut oil, for deep-frying
1 medium red onion (170g), chopped finely
½ cup coarsely chopped fresh coriander
1 tablespoon finely chopped fresh lemon grass
2 fresh small red thai chillies, sliced thinly
2 tablespoons lemon juice
1 teaspoon grated palm sugar
1 tablespoon soy sauce
½ teaspoon sambal oelek
8 small chinese cabbage leaves (360g)

1 Pat tofu with absorbent paper; chop coarsely. Spread tofu, in single layer, on absorbent-paper-lined tray; cover tofu with more absorbent paper, stand at least 20 minutes.

2 Heat oil in wok or large saucepan; deep-fry tofu, in batches, until lightly browned. Drain on absorbent paper.

3 Combine tofu in large bowl with onion, coriander, lemon grass and chilli. Combine juice, sugar, sauce and sambal in small jug; stir until sugar dissolves. Pour dressing over tofu mixture; toss to combine. Serve spooned into individual whole cabbage leaves.

SERVES 4
per serving 27.7g fat; 1641kJ (392 cal)

TIPS

• Larb is a classic Thai dish most usually made of minced beef, chicken or pork and vegetables. Our version is made with the vegetarian's "meat", tofu, with no lessening of fabulous flavour.
• It is important that the tofu is as well drained as possible before it is deep-fried. If you have the time, a few hours before you want to make the larb, pat the whole piece of tofu with absorbent paper, then place it in a strainer or colander lined with absorbent paper set over a large bowl. Weight the tofu piece with an upright saucer topped with a heavy can; allow to drain this way for up to 3 hours. Chop tofu just before deep-frying.
• Peanut oil is good for deep-frying because of its high smoke point (capacity to handle high heat without burning). How much oil to use in the wok for deep-frying depends on what and how much is to be deep-fried: the food must be submerged completely. Do not overfill the wok or saucepan with oil because the level will rise abruptly when the food is added.
• Be careful when deep-frying the tofu; slide rather than drop it into the hot oil to help prevent splattering. Add it in small batches so as not to overcrowd the wok and lower the temperature of the oil.

Pour beaten egg into heated wok and swirl to spread egg evenly to form thin omelette

Cut the fried tofu block into bite-size pieces before reheating it in the wok

The preserved turnip needs to be chopped into fairly small pieces before it is crushed into a paste

vegetarian pad thai

PREPARATION TIME 20 MINUTES (PLUS STANDING TIME) **COOKING TIME** 10 MINUTES

200g rice stick noodles

2 cloves garlic, quartered

2 tablespoons finely chopped preserved turnip

2 fresh small red thai chillies, seeded, chopped coarsely

¼ cup (60ml) peanut oil

2 eggs, beaten lightly

1 cup (90g) fried onion

125g fried tofu, cut into small pieces

¼ cup (35g) coarsely chopped roasted unsalted peanuts

3 cups (240g) bean sprouts

6 green onions, sliced thinly

2 tablespoons soy sauce

1 tablespoon lime juice

2 tablespoons coarsely chopped fresh coriander

1 Place noodles in large heatproof bowl; cover with boiling water, stand until noodles just soften, drain.

2 Meanwhile, using mortar and pestle, crush garlic, turnip and chilli until mixture forms a paste.

3 Heat 2 teaspoons of the oil in wok; pour in egg, swirl wok to make thin omelette. Cook, uncovered, until egg is just set. Remove from wok; roll omelette, cut into thin strips.

4 Heat remaining oil in wok; stir-fry garlic paste and fried onion until fragrant. Add tofu; stir-fry 1 minute. Add half of the nuts, half of the sprouts and half of the green onion; stir-fry until sprouts are just wilted. Add noodles, sauce and juice; stir-fry, tossing gently until combined. Remove from heat; toss remaining nuts, sprouts and green onion with omelette strips and coriander through pad thai. Serve with lime wedges, if desired.

SERVES 4
per serving 27g fat; 1813kJ (433 cal)

TIPS

● Soaking the rice stick noodles (sen lek) in hot water before stir-frying makes them tender and helps prevent them from sticking together. Sen lek are the traditional noodles used in pad thai, and before soaking measure about 5mm in width; other thin rice noodles can be substituted.

● Preserved turnip (hua chai po or cu cai muoi on the label) is also called dried radish because of its similarity to daikon. Sold packaged whole or in slices, it is very salty and needs to be rinsed and dried before use. It is an important ingredient for an authentic pad thai.

● Fried onion, sold in Asian grocery stores packed in jars or in cellophane bags, is used as a topping for various Thai rice and noodle dishes, and also served as a condiment as part of a Thai meal. Fried garlic is sold and used in the same way; both must be kept airtight to remain crisp.

By coring the cauliflower first, you will be able to judge where to cut off the individual florets

Chop the choy sum into even lengths, trimming off only the very bottom of the stems

Roll the lime on a hard surface, pressing down on it, to release as much juice as possible

stir-fried cauliflower, choy sum and snake beans
pad pak ruam

PREPARATION TIME 20 MINUTES   **COOKING TIME** 10 MINUTES

1 tablespoon peanut oil

2 cloves garlic, crushed

1 teaspoon ground turmeric

1 teaspoon finely chopped coriander root and stem mixture

4 green onions, sliced thinly

500g cauliflower florets

¼ cup (60ml) water

200g snake beans, cut into 5cm pieces

200g choy sum, chopped coarsely

1 tablespoon lime juice

1 tablespoon soy sauce

1 tablespoon coarsely chopped fresh coriander

1 Heat oil in wok; cook garlic, turmeric, coriander mixture and onion; stir-fry until onion just softens. Remove from wok; keep warm.

2 Stir-fry cauliflower with the water in same wok until cauliflower is almost tender. Add beans and choy sum; stir-fry until vegetables are just tender.

3 Add juice, sauce, chopped coriander and onion mixture; stir-fry until heated through.

SERVES 4
per serving 5.4g fat; 385kJ (92 cal)

TIPS

● Both the stems and roots of coriander are used in Thai cooking so buy a bunch of fresh coriander with its roots intact. Wash the coriander under cold water, removing any dirt clinging to the roots. Chop roots and stems together and some of the leaves for the tablespoon specified. Freeze the remainder of the chopped root and stem mixture, in teaspoon-size plastic-wrap parcels, for future use.

● You need to buy a piece of cauliflower weighing approximately 1kg to get 500g of florets for this recipe.

● A member of the bok choy family, choy sum (pakaukeo) is easy to identify, with its long stems, light green leaves and yellow flowers (hence its other common name, flowering cabbage). It is eaten stems and all, and is good steamed, on its own, or in a stir-fry.

Lift out and discard the hard strip of centre core from the onion halves

Eat all of the stems of the gai larn: they are actually more flavoursome than its leaves

Remove the thai basil leaves from their stems before chopping them coarsely

stir-fried eggplant tofu   pad makeua tao hu

PREPARATION TIME 15 MINUTES (PLUS STANDING TIME)   **COOKING TIME** 15 MINUTES

1 large eggplant (400g)
300g fresh firm silken tofu
1 medium brown onion (150g)
2 tablespoons peanut oil
1 clove garlic, crushed
2 fresh small red thai chillies, sliced thinly
1 tablespoon grated palm sugar
850g gai larn, chopped coarsely
2 tablespoons lime juice
⅓ cup (80ml) soy sauce
⅓ cup coarsely chopped fresh thai basil

1 Cut unpeeled eggplant in half lengthways; cut each half into thin slices. Place eggplant in colander, sprinkle with salt; stand 30 minutes.

2 Meanwhile, pat tofu all over with absorbent paper; cut into 2cm squares. Spread tofu, in single layer, on absorbent-paper-lined tray; cover tofu with more absorbent paper, stand at least 10 minutes.

3 Cut onion in half, then cut each half into thin even-size wedges. Rinse eggplant under cold water; pat dry with absorbent paper.

4 Heat oil in wok; stir-fry onion, garlic and chilli until onion softens. Add sugar; stir-fry until dissolved. Add eggplant; stir-fry, 1 minute. Add gai larn; stir-fry until just wilted. Add tofu, juice and sauce; stir-fry, tossing gently until combined. Remove from heat; toss basil through stir-fry.

SERVES 4
per serving 15.2g fat; 1071kJ (256 cal)

TIPS

● It is important for the tofu to be as well drained as possible before it is stir-fried. If you have the time, a few hours before you want to make this dish, pat the whole piece of tofu with absorbent paper, then place it in an absorbent-paper-lined strainer or colander set over a large bowl. Weight the tofu piece with an upright saucer topped with a heavy can; allow to drain for up to 3 hours. Cut tofu into squares just before stir-frying.
● Gai larn (kanah), also known as gai lum, chinese broccoli or chinese kale, is appreciated more for its stems than its coarse leaves. It can be served steamed or stir-fried, in soups or in noodle dishes.
● A successful stir-fry needs to be cooked over as high a heat as possible in the briefest amount of time, so it is important that all ingredients are prepared and ready for use before you begin to heat your wok.
● Pour juice and sauce down the side of the wok rather than directly into the centre of the food, so that it is already sizzling by the time it touches the food and thus can't lower the temperature.

Dry, then chop, the pickled galangal coarsely before processing it with the other aromatics into a paste

Cut the zucchini and squash into similar-size pieces so they take the same time to cook

The garlic paste is actually "fried" in the oil released by the boiling coconut milk

mixed vegetables in coconut milk   pak tom kati

PREPARATION TIME 25 MINUTES   **COOKING TIME** 15 MINUTES

6 cloves garlic, quartered

3 fresh small red thai chillies, chopped coarsely

2 tablespoons coarsely chopped fresh lemon grass

1 tablespoon coarsely chopped pickled galangal

20g piece fresh ginger, chopped coarsely

20g piece fresh turmeric, chopped coarsely

2 cups (500ml) coconut milk

2 whole kaffir lime leaves

4 medium zucchini (480g), chopped coarsely

6 yellow patty-pan squash (240g), chopped coarsely

200g cauliflower florets

100g baby corn, halved lengthways

2 tablespoons soy sauce

2 tablespoons lime juice

⅓ cup coarsely chopped fresh thai basil

2 kaffir lime leaves, shredded finely

1 Blend or process (or crush using mortar and pestle) garlic, chilli, lemon grass, galangal, ginger and turmeric until mixture forms a paste.

2 Place half of the coconut milk in wok or large saucepan; bring to a boil. Add garlic paste; whisk over high heat until smooth. Reduce heat, add remaining coconut milk and whole lime leaves; simmer, stirring, until coconut milk mixture thickens slightly.

3 Add zucchini, squash, cauliflower and corn; bring to a boil. Reduce heat; simmer, uncovered, about 5 minutes or until vegetables are just tender. Remove from heat; remove and discard whole lime leaves. Stir sauce, juice and basil into vegetable mixture; serve topped with shredded lime leaves.

SERVES 4
per serving 26.9g fat; 1406kJ (336 cal)

TIPS

● This vegetable recipe is a good example of a typical Thai curry from the south of the country, where the food bears the closest similarities to the food of India. The chilli, turmeric, ginger and coconut milk could just as easily be found in a southern Indian vegetable curry as they are in this.
● You need a piece of cauliflower weighing about 400g to get enough florets for this recipe.

● Turmeric (kamin), a rhizome related to galangal and ginger, must be grated or pounded to release its somewhat acrid aroma and pungent flavour. Known for the golden colour it bestows on the dishes in which it's used, fresh turmeric can be substituted with the more common dried powder (use 2 teaspoons of ground turmeric plus 1 teaspoon of sugar for every 20g of fresh turmeric called for in a recipe).

● Peel and cut any remaining fresh turmeric and ginger into 20g pieces, then wrap individually in plastic and freeze for future use. They'll keep for months and are easier to grate when frozen.
● Pickled galangal (ka dong) is used both in cooking and as a condiment to be served with various dishes. It is sold in jars or cryovac-packed in Asian grocery stores. You can substitute pickled ginger but the taste will differ.

Remove the leaves from the stems of opal basil carefully without tearing or bruising

Before using the sugar snap peas, pull away the chewy string that runs along one side

Remove onion with a slotted spoon so oil falls back into the wok for the rest of deep-frying

pumpkin, basil and chilli stir-fry pad pet fak tong

PREPARATION TIME 10 MINUTES **COOKING TIME** 15 MINUTES

⅓ cup (80ml) peanut oil
1 large brown onion (200g), sliced thinly
2 cloves garlic, sliced thinly
4 fresh small red thai chillies, sliced thinly
1kg pumpkin, chopped coarsely
250g sugar snap peas
1 teaspoon grated palm sugar
¼ cup (60ml) vegetable stock (page 117)
2 tablespoons soy sauce
¾ cup loosely packed opal basil leaves
4 green onions, sliced thinly
½ cup (75g) roasted unsalted peanuts

1 Heat oil in wok; cook brown onion, in batches, until browned and crisp. Drain on absorbent paper.
2 Stir-fry garlic and chilli in wok until fragrant. Add pumpkin; stir-fry until browned all over and just tender. Add peas, sugar, stock and sauce; stir-fry until sauce thickens slightly.
3 Remove from heat; toss basil, green onion and nuts through stir-fry until well combined. Serve topped with fried onion.

SERVES 4
per serving 20.7g fat; 1436kJ (343 cal)

TIPS

● Opal basil has purple leaves and a sweet, almost gingery, flavour. It has better keeping properties than most other basils, and it can be used interchangeably with thai basil in recipes such as this to add its striking colour and flavour to the finished dish. Try frying off a dozen or so of the whole opal basil leaves in the heated oil before

you fry the onion slices. Drain them on absorbent paper and then sprinkle over the finished dish just before serving.
● We have not seeded the chillies in this recipe. If you want your stir-fry to be milder, remove the seeds before frying the chillies.
● If you would like to make this vegetable stir-fry even hotter, slice the

unseeded red chillies into long strips and fry them in the oil at the beginning of the recipe with the brown onion until they are crisp and almost blackened. Their heat is incredible but their colour, crunch and taste are sublime.
● Whole roasted unsalted cashews can be substituted for the peanuts.

Remove as much of the bitter white pith as possible when peeling the pomelos

Remove the membrane around each pomelo segment and as many of the seeds as you can

Roast the whole peanuts in a heated wok, stirring constantly to ensure they don't scorch

pomelo salad yum som-o

PREPARATION TIME 30 MINUTES

1 small red onion (100g)
4 large pomelos (4kg)
2 green onions, sliced thinly
2 fresh small red thai chillies, sliced thinly
¼ cup coarsely chopped fresh coriander
½ cup (70g) coarsely chopped roasted
  unsalted peanuts
2 cloves garlic, crushed
1 tablespoon grated palm sugar
¼ cup (60ml) lime juice
1 tablespoon soy sauce

1 Halve red onion; cut each half into paper-thin wedges.
2 Peel and carefully segment pomelos; discard membranes. Combine segments in large bowl with onions, chilli, coriander and nuts.
3 Combine remaining ingredients in small jug; stir until sugar dissolves. Pour dressing over pomelo mixture; toss gently to combine.

SERVES 4
per serving 10.6g fat; 1311kJ (313 cal)

TIPS

● One of the many interesting things about Thai cooking is the use of tropical or unusual fruits in its main courses, salads or side dishes. Banana, mango, pawpaw and pomelo are just a few of the fruits that find their way out of the dessert fruit platter. Here, where pomelo is married with peanuts and splashed with a tart, garlicky dressing, you'll experience a wonderful taste sensation outside the realm of Western familiarity but one which is delightfully more-ish.
● Similar to a grapefruit in many ways, a pomelo is sweeter, somewhat more conical in shape and slightly larger, about the size of a small coconut. Its firm rind allows it to be peeled easily and neatly, like a mandarin, and the segments can be easily separated from one another. A pomelo can be used in place of grapefruit in most recipes, and you can substitute grapefruit here if pomelo is out of season.
● Grated cabbage and shredded mint leaves can be tossed into this salad for a heartier main course.

Peel and devein the prawns but leave the tails intact when using in this salad

Soak the noodles in a heatproof bowl filled with boiling water until they are just softened

Use kitchen scissors to cut the softened noodles into random lengths while they are draining

cold prawn salad yum goong wun sen

PREPARATION TIME 20 MINUTES (PLUS STANDING TIME)

200g bean thread noodles

1 clove garlic, crushed

2 tablespoons fish sauce

1 tablespoon lime juice

2 teaspoons peanut oil

¼ cup (35g) coarsely chopped roasted unsalted peanuts

2 green onions, sliced thinly

¼ cup coarsely chopped fresh coriander

2 fresh small red thai chillies, seeded, sliced thinly

1kg large cooked king prawns, peeled, deveined

1 Place noodles in large heatproof bowl; cover with boiling water. Stand until just tender; drain. Using kitchen scissors, cut noodles into random lengths.

2 Whisk garlic, sauce, juice and oil in large bowl to combine.

3 Add noodles to bowl with nuts, onion, coriander, chilli and prawns; toss gently to combine.

SERVES 4
per serving 7.8g fat; 1353kJ (323 cal)

TIPS

● This superb traditional Thai salad should only be made just before you want to serve it, but you can have most of the ingredients prepared and ready to go: chop the peanuts and coriander; slice the green onion; peel and devein the prawns, squeeze the lime and so forth. But neither soak the noodles nor toss everything together until mealtime.

● Bean thread noodles (wun sen), made from mung beans, are also called cellophane or glass noodles because they are transparent when cooked. They usually come dried in bundles and are white in colour (not off-white like rice vermicelli). Soak them only until they become soft – any longer and they become stodgy or start to fragment. Drain them when they become opaque; they only become transparent if they are cooked further. Alternatively, they can be deep-fried without pre-soaking.

● Thai chillies (sometimes referred to as "scuds") are especially fiery – if you want to decrease their heat, seed them before chopping. When doing so, always wear disposable kitchen gloves because they can burn your skin.

Cut the cooked fish into pieces small enough to allow it to be processed into a fine consistency

Remove crisp fish from the wok with a slotted spoon, then spread it on absorbent paper

Freeze any remaining grated lime rind, sealed in a plastic bag, for future use

crisp fish salad with chilli lime dressing   yum pla foo

PREPARATION TIME 20 MINUTES **COOKING TIME** 30 MINUTES

250g firm white fish fillets
vegetable oil, for deep-frying
1 medium red onion (170g), sliced thinly
6 green onions, sliced thinly
2 lebanese cucumbers (260g), seeded, sliced thinly
1 cup firmly packed thai mint leaves
1 cup firmly packed coriander leaves
2 tablespoons coarsely chopped roasted unsalted peanuts
2 teaspoons finely grated lime rind

CHILLI LIME DRESSING
4 fresh small green thai chillies, seeded, chopped finely
2 tablespoons fish sauce
⅓ cup (80ml) lime juice
1 tablespoon brown sugar

1 Preheat oven to moderate. Place fish on wire rack over oven tray; roast, uncovered, 20 minutes. When cool enough to handle, cut fish into pieces, then blend or process, pulsing, until mixture resembles coarse breadcrumbs.

2 Heat oil in wok or deep frying pan; deep-fry processed fish, in batches, until lightly browned and crisp. Drain on absorbent paper.

3 Combine onions, cucumber and herbs in large bowl; add chilli lime dressing, toss to combine. Sprinkle salad with crisp fish, nuts and lime rind; serve immediately.
chilli lime dressing Combine ingredients in screw-top jar; shake well.

SERVES 4
per serving 7.1g fat; 711kJ (170 cal)

TIPS

• A splendid example of a quintessential Thai dish, the salad or appetiser yum pla foo plays the four main flavours (sweet, sour, salty and spicy) against one another while neatly balancing a variety of textures.
• We used ling for this recipe but you can use any boneless firm white fish fillet – blue-eye, swordfish or sea perch are all good choices. Check for any small pieces of bone in the fillets and use tweezers to remove them. Salting

your fingers helps you get a better grip when pulling away any skin from the fillet. When topping the salad, rub fish between your hands to make it an even finer consistency, letting it "rain" over the other ingredients.
• You don't need much oil to deep-fry this amount of pulverised fish (and, remember, you should fry it in small batches so it doesn't clump together into a ball), so there's no need to cool and keep it, as we've recommended in

other recipes calling for deep-frying.
• Thai mint (saranae) is also known as marsh mint, and is similar to spearmint. Its somewhat thick round leaves are usually used raw, as a flavouring to be sprinkled over soups and salads.
• You can freeze any remaining grated lime rind, sealed in a small plastic bag, so you have some to hand should you run out of limes. Fresh limes can be frozen whole so buy them in quantity when in season, plentiful and cheap.

While draining the crab, use kitchen tweezers to remove any remnant shell

Using a sharp, heavy knife, slice the chinese cabbage leaves into fine shreds

After halving the cucumber, scoop out and discard the seeds using the rim of the bowl of a teaspoon

crab salad   yum pla-puu

PREPARATION TIME 15 MINUTES

500g fresh crab meat
250g chinese cabbage, chopped finely
1 lebanese cucumber (130g), seeded, chopped coarsely
1 medium red onion (170g), halved, sliced thinly
6 green onions, cut into 4cm lengths
1 cup loosely packed fresh thai mint leaves

DRESSING
2 cloves garlic, crushed
2 tablespoons lime juice
2 tablespoons fish sauce
1 tablespoon brown sugar
2 fresh small red thai chillies, chopped finely

1 Drain crab in strainer; remove any shell and if necessary shred the meat to desired texture.
2 Combine crab in large bowl with cabbage, cucumber, onions and mint; pour in dressing, toss to combine.
dressing Combine all ingredients in screw-top jar; shake well.

SERVES 4
per serving 1g fat; 529kJ (126 cal)

TIPS

● Thai mint (saranae) is also known as marsh mint, and is similar to spearmint. Its somewhat thick round leaves are usually used raw, as a flavouring to be sprinkled over soups and salads. You can substitute ordinary garden mint for it, but the taste of the finished salad will not be exactly the same.
● If preferred, substitute 500g cooked shelled medium prawns for the crab.

● Chinese cabbage, also known as peking or napa cabbage, wong bok or petsai, is elongated in shape and has pale green, crinkly leaves. A fairly bland-tasting cabbage, it is the most commonly used variety throughout all of South-East Asia, forming the basis of the pickled Korean condiment, kim chi, and providing the crunch in fresh vietnamese rice paper rolls.

● Seed the unpeeled cucumbers for this salad before chopping them by scooping down the length of a cut half with the rim of the bowl of a teaspoon; rinse and pat dry with absorbent paper. If you like, you can do this an hour or so before you assemble the salad, thus allowing the seeded cucumber halves to drain, cut-side down on absorbent paper, before chopping them.

Discard liquid inside the can of lychees, then rinse the fruit under cold water and allow to drain

After the cooked pork has rested, slice it thinly before marinating it in the pickled garlic dressing

Stack the kaffir lime leaves, roll them tightly, then slice across the cylinder into very thin shreds

pork and lychee salad yum muu lynchee

PREPARATION TIME 20 MINUTES (PLUS STANDING TIME) **COOKING TIME** 10 MINUTES

1 tablespoon peanut oil

300g pork fillet

565g can lychees, rinsed, drained, halved

1 medium red capsicum (200g), sliced thinly

1 stick fresh lemon grass, sliced thinly

2 fresh kaffir lime leaves, shredded finely

100g watercress

2 tablespoons coarsely chopped fresh vietnamese mint

2 tablespoons drained thinly sliced pickled ginger

2 tablespoons fried shallot

PICKLED GARLIC DRESSING

1 tablespoon drained finely chopped pickled garlic

2 fresh small red thai chillies, seeded, sliced thinly

1 tablespoon rice vinegar

1 tablespoon lime juice

1 tablespoon fish sauce

1 tablespoon palm sugar

1 Heat oil in wok; cook pork, turning, until browned all over and cooked as desired. Cover, stand 10 minutes; slice thinly. Place pork in medium bowl with pickled garlic dressing; toss to coat pork all over. Stand 10 minutes.

2 Meanwhile, combine lychees, capsicum, lemon grass, lime leaves, watercress and mint in large bowl.

3 Add pork mixture to lychee mixture; toss gently to combine. Serve sprinkled with pickled ginger and fried shallot.
pickled garlic dressing Combine all ingredients in screw-top jar; shake well.

SERVES 4
per serving 7.4g fat; 920kJ (220 cal)

TIPS

● We rinsed and drained a 565g can of lychees for this recipe but, if fresh lychees are available, substitute 300g of these, halved and peeled. You can also use rambutans or longans in this salad.
● Fried shallot (homm jiew) and fried garlic (kratiem jiew) are usually served as condiments or sprinkled on top of just-cooked dishes. Both can be found at Asian grocery stores; once opened, they keep for months if tightly sealed.

● Sweet and subtle pickled garlic, or kratiem dong, is the young green bulb, pickled whole and unpeeled in vinegar brine and packed in jars. Eaten as a snack in Thailand, it can be served as a condiment to be sprinkled over salads or noodle dishes, or used in a dressing, as here. Pickled ginger (khing dong) is used both in cooking and as a condiment. It is sold by the jar or cryovac-packed in Asian grocery stores.

Wear disposable kitchen gloves to slice chillies; leave one unseeded for more heat

Traditionally the beef is grilled to medium-rare; it will feel slightly resistant when touched

After the meat has rested but is still warm, slice it into extremely fine slices against the grain

char-grilled beef salad   yum nuah

PREPARATION TIME 15 MINUTES (PLUS MARINATING TIME) **COOKING TIME** 10 MINUTES

500g beef rump steak
¼ cup (60ml) fish sauce
¼ cup (60ml) lime juice
3 lebanese cucumbers (390g), seeded, sliced thinly
4 fresh small red thai chillies, sliced thinly
8 green onions, sliced thinly
250g cherry tomatoes, quartered
1 cup loosely packed vietnamese mint leaves
1 cup loosely packed coriander leaves
1 tablespoon grated palm sugar
2 teaspoons soy sauce
1 clove garlic, crushed

1 Combine beef with 2 tablespoons of the fish sauce and 1 tablespoon of the juice in large bowl; cover, refrigerate 3 hours or overnight.

2 Drain beef; discard marinade. Cook beef on heated oiled grill plate (or grill or barbecue) until browned both sides and cooked as desired. Cover, stand 5 minutes; slice thinly.

3 Meanwhile, combine cucumber, chilli, onion, tomato and herbs in large bowl. Combine remaining juice and fish sauce with sugar, soy sauce and garlic in screw-top jar; shake well.

4 Add beef and dressing to salad; toss gently to combine.

SERVES 4
per serving 8.7g fat; 1008kJ (241 cal)

TIPS

● Slicing the onion and cucumber as thinly as possible maximises their individual flavours once the salad is tossed together.
● You can use beef eye fillet or scotch fillet in place of rump. For authenticity, we cooked our beef to barely-medium-rare; adjust cooking time to suit your taste. To avoid toughening the beef, never turn it more than once during cooking. Standing the beef allows the meat to "relax" and the juices to "settle", making slicing easier.

● Any type of tomato can be used in place of the cherry tomatoes; cut into bite-size pieces. Some larger tomatoes should be seeded first because the seeds and juice will dilute the dressing and make the salad too wet.
● We used the Thai fish sauce, naam pla, but the Vietnamese version, nuoc naam, is very similar; sometimes the bottle will read fish "gravy" but it is the same pungent liquid inside. Adjust the amount of fish sauce to suit your taste. Start with less than we've stated, then

gradually add more until the desired intensity is achieved. The taste of this salad should be balanced between the flavour of the fish sauce and the lime juice; add more or less of either until you are happy with the taste.
● It's best to make the salad close to serving. The beef should still be slightly warm and the vegetables and herbs crisp.
● The salad dressing can be made a day ahead and kept, covered, in the refrigerator.

Stir the rice constantly in a hot dry wok so that it is "roasted" without burning

Pulverise the lightly browned rice into a fine powder using your mortar and pestle

Cut the core out of the lettuce, then pound on a kitchen bench to loosen the whole leaves

spicy chicken salad   larb gai

PREPARATION TIME 25 MINUTES   **COOKING TIME** 20 MINUTES

2 tablespoons long-grain white rice

1 tablespoon peanut oil

1 tablespoon finely chopped fresh lemon grass

2 fresh small red thai chillies, seeded, chopped finely

2 cloves garlic, crushed

1 tablespoon finely chopped fresh galangal

750g chicken mince

1 lebanese cucumber (130g), seeded, sliced thinly

1 small red onion (100g), sliced thinly

100g bean sprouts

½ cup loosely packed fresh thai basil leaves

1 cup loosely packed fresh coriander leaves

4 large iceberg lettuce leaves

DRESSING

⅓ cup (80ml) lime juice

2 tablespoons fish sauce

2 tablespoons kecap manis

2 tablespoons peanut oil

2 teaspoons grated palm sugar

½ teaspoon sambal oelek

1 Heat dry wok; stir-fry rice until lightly browned. Blend or process (or crush using mortar and pestle) rice until it resembles fine breadcrumbs.

2 Heat oil in same wok; stir-fry lemon grass, chilli, garlic and galangal until fragrant. Remove from wok. Stir-fry chicken, in batches, until changed in colour and cooked through.

3 Return chicken and lemon grass mixture to wok with about ⅓ of the dressing; stir-fry about 5 minutes or until mixture thickens slightly.

4 Place remaining dressing in large bowl with chicken, cucumber, onion, sprouts and herbs; toss gently to combine. Place lettuce leaves on serving plates; divide larb salad among leaves, sprinkle with ground rice.
dressing Combine all ingredients in screw-top jar; shake well.

SERVES 4
per serving 29.7g fat; 1997kJ (477 cal)

TIPS

● Remove the core from an iceberg lettuce; with the core-end facing up, smash the lettuce down hard on your kitchen bench to help loosen the outermost leaves so that they fall away without tearing.
● Thai basil (horapa) is different from the ordinary sweet basil. It has a distinct anise flavour, small leaves and purple stems. It is easy to grow from seed: choose a sunny spot, and pick often to encourage growth.

● Sieu wan is the Thai term for the dark, thick, sweet soy sauce that is here called by its more familiar Indonesian and Malaysian name, kecap manis.
● Fresh thai chillies (prik ki noo) are also known as scuds or birds-eye chillies and are one of the hottest varieties. Any small red chillies can be used instead (to increase the heat, don't seed them).
● We used sambal oelek but you can use hot vietnamese chilli paste or, for less heat, mild sweet thai chilli sauce.

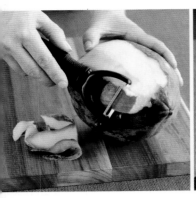

Peel the papaya still whole, then rinse under cold water and pat dry before cutting it

Grate the seeded papaya into very thin strips using the largest holes of a grater

Chop dried shrimp with a heavy knife until as fine as possible before measuring the required amount

green papaya salad   som tum

PREPARATION TIME 25 MINUTES   **COOKING TIME** 3 MINUTES

100g snake beans

850g green papaya

250g cherry tomatoes, quartered

3 fresh small green thai chillies, seeded, chopped finely

2 tablespoons finely chopped dried shrimp

¼ cup (60ml) lime juice

1 tablespoon fish sauce

1 tablespoon grated palm sugar

2 cloves garlic, crushed

¼ cup coarsely chopped fresh coriander

2 cups (120g) finely shredded iceberg lettuce

⅓ cup (50g) coarsely chopped roasted unsalted peanuts

1 Cut beans in 5cm pieces; cut pieces in half lengthways. Boil, steam or microwave beans until just tender; drain. Rinse immediately under cold water; drain.

2 Meanwhile, peel papaya. Quarter lengthways, remove seeds; grate papaya coarsely.

3 Place papaya and beans in large bowl with tomato, chilli and shrimp. Add combined juice, sauce, sugar, garlic and half of the coriander; toss gently to combine.

4 Place lettuce on serving plates; spoon papaya salad over lettuce, sprinkle with nuts and remaining coriander.

SERVES 4
per serving 7g fat; 677kJ (162 cal)

TIPS

● There are many ways to make green papaya salads, with varying degrees of hotness, sourness and sweetness. The hottest variety is made in north-eastern Thailand and Laos where, eaten with barbecued chicken and sticky rice, it is part of the staple diet. There, the salads are made by bruising sliced green papaya with garlic and hot red chillies (prik ki noo), then adding lime juice, tamarind and other flavourings.

● Green (unripe) papayas are readily available in various sizes at many Asian shops and markets. Select one that is very hard and slightly shiny, which indicates that it is freshly picked. It's imperative that it be totally unripe, the flesh so light green it is almost white. Buy the firmest one you can find: it will soften rapidly if you don't use it within one or two days.

● Green papaya has very little taste itself but acts as a sponge to absorb the combined Thai flavours (hot, sour, sweet and salty) of the other ingredients. Assemble the salad just before you want to serve it, otherwise the papaya will lose its crisp texture.

● Some people are sensitive to the sap of green papaya, so the first time you make this salad you might like to wear disposable kitchen gloves when peeling and seeding the fruit. Many cooks suggest rinsing the papaya halves in cold water, then drying them well to remove any traces of this sap.

curry pastes

Much of Thai food has its roots in cuisines native to the many traders and immigrants who arrived in Thailand in the distant past, and one of these influences came from southern India. Indian curries evolved from being just condiments to add to the main meal of rice, to the many different robust dishes we are familiar with today. Since rice has always been an indispensable part of the Thai table, the concept of various sauces created intentionally to add different savoury flavours to rice was the original basis of many Thai curry pastes. And the coconut milk used in southern Indian curries to season, thicken and serve as a chilli-tempering foil happily found its niche in the Thai kitchen.

tips & techniques

Thai curries are made from far more than just a blend of dried spices or the ubiquitous canned yellow powder with which we are all familiar. A Thai curry paste is an amalgam of fresh herbs, aromatic spices, dried and fresh chillies, fruits, seafood, stems, roots and shoots, smashed or ground together in various proportions to make complex-tasting, intensely flavoured pastes.

Traditionally, curry paste is made with a mortar and pestle but, for ease and speed, we made our paste recipes in a blender or food processor. If your machine cannot break down the ingredients' fibrous content into a smooth paste, we suggest that you first pulverise them in a blender or processor until they become pulpy, then transfer the mixture to a mortar and pestle for a final grinding. However you decide to make a curry paste, you should aim for a result that is thick but not lumpy, to guarantee homogeneity of flavour.

There are many bottled and canned curry pastes available at Asian food stores and your local supermarket,

some imported from Thailand while others are made locally, and, if you don't have time to make one, these commercial pastes will do the job.

However, if it's authenticity you're after, only a homemade curry paste gives you that complex but harmonious blend of the four distinct tastes inherent to the food of Thailand – sweet, salty, spicy and sour (and, to a lesser degree, a fifth, bitter).

Since they keep well, curry pastes can be prepared in quantity so you have plenty at hand for future use. Each recipe on the following pages makes a cup of curry paste, more than is required for any one recipe, so you'll have them ready and waiting whenever you next want to cook Thai food.

Use what you need at the time, then place the remaining paste in a glass jar, cover it tightly and refrigerate it for up to a week. A better idea is to make the paste, use what you want for that occasion, then freeze the rest. Place tablespoons of curry paste in the compartments of an ice-cube tray; wrap the tray tightly in plastic wrap and

put it in your freezer until the paste solidifies. Remove the blocks of curry paste, then re-wrap them individually and return to the freezer until required. This way you'll never need to thaw more than you need at any given time. You can store curry pastes this way for up to three months with no discernible difference in flavour.

We've given recipes for a handful of the most popular curry pastes but, once you've experimented with these, don't feel locked into our formulas forever. Add to, alter or delete ingredients according to your taste preferences. Like garlic? Double what we suggest. Afraid of too much chilli? Gradually decrease the amounts suggested.

Curry pastes are, as the name implies, an essential ingredient in the making of a Thai curry, but they can be used in any number of other dishes, from stir-fries and salads to soups and marinades. Every dish you add them to, no matter how quickly it's prepared, will taste as though it's been slowly simmered for hours, such is its depth and complexity of flavour.

curry pastes

With the exception of the massaman paste (which, like its Indian forebears, takes about 15 minutes in a hot oven to dry-roast the spices), these recipes only take a little cooking time, and will keep, covered tightly, in the refrigerator for up to a week. See our tips on the previous page for freezing curry pastes. Each recipe makes 1 cup (300g) curry paste.

red curry paste
gaeng ped

PREPARATION TIME 20 MINUTES
(PLUS STANDING TIME)
COOKING TIME 3 MINUTES

20 dried long red chillies
1 teaspoon ground coriander
2 teaspoons ground cumin
1 teaspoon hot paprika
2 teaspoons finely chopped
   fresh ginger
3 large cloves garlic, quartered
1 medium (170g) red onion,
   chopped coarsely
2 sticks fresh lemon grass,
   sliced thinly
1 fresh kaffir lime leaf,
   sliced thinly
2 tablespoons coarsely chopped
   fresh coriander root and
   stem mixture
2 teaspoons shrimp paste
1 tablespoon peanut oil

1 Place whole chillies in small
   heatproof jug, cover with boiling
   water; stand 15 minutes, drain.
2 Meanwhile, stir ground coriander,
   cumin and paprika over medium
   heat in small dry-heated frying
   pan until fragrant.
3 Blend or process chillies and
   roasted spices with remaining
   ingredients, except for the oil,
   until mixture forms a paste,
   pausing to scrape down
   sides of machine occasionally
   during blending.
4 Add oil to paste mixture; continue
   to blend in machine or using
   mortar and pestle until smooth.

green curry paste
gaeng keow wahn

PREPARATION TIME 20 MINUTES
COOKING TIME 3 MINUTES

2 teaspoons ground coriander
2 teaspoons ground cumin
10 fresh long green chillies,
   chopped coarsely
10 fresh small green chillies,
   chopped coarsely
1 large clove garlic, quartered
4 green onions, chopped coarsely
1 stick fresh lemon grass,
   sliced thinly
2 fresh kaffir lime leaves,
   sliced thinly
1 teaspoon finely chopped
   fresh galangal
¼ cup coarsely chopped fresh
   coriander root and stem mixture
1 teaspoon shrimp paste
1 tablespoon peanut oil

1 Stir ground coriander and cumin
   in small dry-heated frying pan
   over medium heat until fragrant.
2 Blend or process roasted spices
   with remaining ingredients,
   except for the oil, until mixture
   forms a paste, pausing to
   scrape down sides of machine
   occasionally during blending.
3 Add oil to paste mixture; continue
   to blend in machine or using
   mortar and pestle until smooth.

massaman curry paste
gaeng masaman

PREPARATION TIME 15 MINUTES
(PLUS STANDING TIME)
COOKING TIME 20 MINUTES

20 dried long red chillies
1 teaspoon ground coriander
2 teaspoons ground cumin
2 teaspoons ground cinnamon
½ teaspoon ground cardamom
½ teaspoon ground clove
5 large cloves garlic, quartered
1 large (200g) brown onion,
   chopped coarsely
2 sticks fresh lemon grass,
   sliced thinly
3 fresh kaffir lime leaves,
   sliced thinly
1 tablespoon coarsely chopped
   fresh ginger
2 teaspoons shrimp paste
1 tablespoon peanut oil

1 Preheat oven to moderate. Place
   chillies in small heatproof jug,
   cover with boiling water; stand
   15 minutes, drain.
2 Meanwhile, combine ground
   coriander, cumin, cinnamon,
   cardamom and clove in small
   dry-heated frying pan; stir over
   medium heat until fragrant.
3 Place chillies and roasted spices
   in small shallow baking dish with
   remaining ingredients. Roast,
   uncovered, in moderate oven
   for 15 minutes.
4 Blend or process roasted curry
   paste mixture, or crush, using
   mortar and pestle, until smooth.

panang curry paste
gaeng panaeng

PREPARATION TIME 20 MINUTES
(PLUS STANDING TIME)
COOKING TIME 3 MINUTES

25 dried long red chillies
1 teaspoon ground coriander
2 teaspoons ground cumin
2 large cloves garlic, quartered
8 green onions, chopped coarsely
2 sticks fresh lemon grass,
  sliced thinly
2 teaspoons finely chopped
  fresh galangal
2 teaspoons shrimp paste
½ cup (75g) roasted
  unsalted peanuts
2 tablespoons peanut oil

1 Place chillies in small heatproof
  jug, cover with boiling water;
  stand 15 minutes, drain.
2 Meanwhile, stir ground
  coriander and cumin over
  medium heat in small dry-heated
  frying pan until fragrant.
3 Blend or process chillies and
  roasted spices with remaining
  ingredients, except for the oil,
  until mixture forms a paste,
  pausing to scrape down sides
  of machine occasionally
  during blending.
4 Add oil to paste mixture; continue
  to blend in machine or using
  mortar and pestle until smooth.

yellow curry paste
gaeng leuang

PREPARATION TIME 20 MINUTES
COOKING TIME 3 MINUTES

1 teaspoon ground coriander
1 teaspoon ground cumin
½ teaspoon ground cinnamon
1 teaspoon finely chopped
  fresh turmeric
5 fresh long yellow chillies,
  chopped coarsely
2 large cloves garlic, quartered
1 medium (150g) brown onion,
  chopped coarsely
2 tablespoons finely chopped
  fresh lemon grass
2 teaspoons finely chopped
  fresh galangal
1 tablespoon coarsely chopped
  fresh coriander root and
  stem mixture
1 teaspoon shrimp paste
1 tablespoon peanut oil

1 Stir ground coriander, cumin
  and cinnamon over medium
  heat in small dry-heated frying
  pan until fragrant.
2 Blend or process roasted spices
  with remaining ingredients,
  except for the oil, until mixture
  forms a paste, pausing to
  scrape down sides of machine
  occasionally during blending.
3 Add oil to paste mixture; continue
  to blend in machine or using
  mortar and pestle until smooth.

It's a good idea to have all the ingredients ready for use before you start to process the paste

Dry-fry the various spices in a small frying pan in order to bring out their dormant flavours

To achieve a smooth curry paste, finish blending the ingredients with a mortar and pestle

glossary

basil

HOLY also known as kra pao or hot basil, is different from thai basil (horapa) and the familiar sweet basil used in Italian cooking; has an almost hot, spicy flavour similar to clove, and is used in cooking many Thai dishes, especially curries. Can be distinguished from horapa by the tiny "hairs" on its leaves and stems.

THAI also known as horapa, is different from holy basil and sweet basil in both look and taste. Having smaller leaves and purplish stems, it has a slight liquorice or aniseed taste, and is one of the basic flavours that typify Thai cuisine.

OPAL has large purple leaves and a sweet, almost gingery flavour. It can be used instead of thai but not holy basil in recipes.

bok choy also known as bak choy, pak choi, chinese white cabbage or chinese chard, has a fresh, mild mustard taste; use stems and leaves, stir-fry or braise.

capsicum also known as bell pepper or, simply, pepper. Seeds and membranes should be discarded before use; comes in several colours, each of which has an individual flavour.

chilli

GREEN generally unripened thai chillies but sometimes different naturally green varieties such as jalapeño or serrano chillies.

PASTE every Asian cuisine has its own chilli paste, and each is different from the next. We used a hot Vietnamese chilli paste in this book but you can use Indonesian sambal oelek (chilli with ginger, oil and garlic) or, for less heat, mild sweet thai chilli sauce, made with vinegar and sugar.

SAUCE if not specified as sweet, we used a hot Chinese variety made of chillies, soy and vinegar; use sparingly, increasing amounts to taste.

SWEET CHILLI SAUCE Thai in origin, a comparatively mild, thin sauce made from red chillies, sugar, garlic and vinegar; used as a condiment more often than in cooking.

THAI bright red to dark green in colour, ranging in size from small ("scuds") to long and thin; among the hottest of chillies.

chinese barbecued duck traditionally cooked in special ovens, this duck has a sweet-sticky coating made from soy sauce, sherry, five-spice and hoisin sauce. It is available from Asian food stores.

chinese cabbage also known as peking or napa cabbage, wong bok or petsai. Elongated in shape with pale green, crinkly leaves, this is the most common cabbage in South-East Asia, forming the basis of the pickled Korean condiment, kim chi, and providing the crunch in vietnamese rice paper rolls. Can be shredded or chopped and eaten raw or braised, steamed or stir-fried.

chives long, very fine green leaves usually eaten uncooked; related to the onion and leek, with subtle onion flavour.

FLOWERING have rougher leaves than simple chives, with a teardrop-shaped pink bud at the top; used in salads or steamed and eaten as vegetable.

GARLIC also known as chinese chives; are strongly flavoured, have flat leaves and are eaten as a vegetable, usually in stir-fries.

choy sum also known as pakaukeo or flowering cabbage, a member of the bok choy family; easy to identify with its long stems and yellow flowers. Can be eaten, stems and all, steamed or stir-fried.

coconut milk/cream not the juice found inside the fruit, but liquid pressed from the white meat of a mature coconut. After the liquid settles, the cream and "milk" (thin white fluid) separate naturally. Coconut cream is obtained commercially from the first pressing of the coconut flesh alone, without the addition of water; the second pressing (less rich) is sold as the milk.

coriander (pak chee) also known as cilantro; bright-green-leafed herb with a pungent flavour. Often stirred into a dish just before serving for maximum impact. The stems and roots are also used in Thai cooking; wash well before chopping.

curry pastes

GREEN the hottest of the traditional pastes; particularly good in chicken and vegetable curries, also in stir-fries and noodle dishes.

MASSAMAN has a spicy flavour reminiscent of Middle-Eastern cooking; favoured by southern Thai Muslim communities for use in hot stew-like curries and satay sauces.

PANANG based on the curries of Penang, an island off the north-west coast of Malaysia, close to the Thai border. A complex, sweet and milder variation of red curry paste; good with seafood and for adding to soups and salad dressings.

RED probably the most popular curry paste; a hot blend of different flavours that complements the richness of pork, duck and seafood, also works well in marinades and sauces.

YELLOW one of the mildest pastes; similar to Indian curry due to use of yellow chillies and fresh turmeric. Good used with coconut in vegetable, rice and noodle dishes.

dried shrimp (goong hang) salted sun-dried prawns ranging in size from not much larger than a grain of rice to "big" ones measuring about 1cm in length. They are sold packaged, shelled, in all Asian grocery stores.

eggplant also known as aubergine. Ranging in size from tiny to very large and in colour from pale green to deep purple, eggplant has an equally wide variety of flavours.

PEA (makeua puong) slightly larger than a green pea and of similar shape and colour; sold fresh, in bunches like grapes, or pickled packed in jars. More bitter than the slightly larger thai eggplant, with which it can be substituted in many Thai recipes; both can be found in Asian grocery stores.

THAI (makeua prao) golf-ball-sized eggplants available in different colours but most commonly green traced in off-white; crisper than the common purple Western variety, they have bitter seeds that must be removed before using.

fish sauce called naam pla if it is Thai made; the Vietnamese version, nuoc naam, is almost identical. Made from pulverised salted fermented fish (most often anchovies); has a pungent smell and strong taste.

fried garlic (kratiem jiew) sold in Asian grocery stores packed in jars or in cellophane bags; used as a topping for various Thai rice and noodle dishes, and also as a condiment for a Thai meal.

gai larn (kanah) also known as gai lum, chinese broccoli or chinese kale; appreciated more for its stems than its coarse leaves. Can be served steamed and stir-fried, in soups and noodle dishes.

galangal (ka) a rhizome with a hot ginger-citrusy flavour; used similarly to ginger and garlic as a seasoning and as an

114

ingredient. Sometimes known as thai or siamese ginger, it also comes in a dried powdered form called laos. Fresh ginger can be substituted but the flavour of the dish will not be the same.

PICKLED (ka dong) is used both in cooking and as a condiment served with various noodle and chicken dishes. It is sold cryovac-packed or in jars in Asian grocery stores. You can substitute pickled ginger but the taste will not be exactly the same.

green papaya readily available in various sizes at many Asian shops and markets; look for one that is very hard and slightly shiny. For use in Thai cooking, papaya must be totally unripe, the flesh so light green it is almost white. Buy the firmest one you can find; it will soften rapidly within a day or so.

ka chai sometimes spelled krachai or kah chi, also known as lesser galangal, chinese ginger or finger-root; long, brown fingerling-like roots available fresh, dried, canned or pickled in brine. Similar to ginger in flavour with a slight hint of camphor, it is found in Asian supermarkets and greengrocers.

kaffir lime (magrood) also known as jeruk purut; bumpy-skinned, wrinkled green fruit of a small citrus tree originally grown in South Africa and South-East Asia. Its zest gives Thai food its unique aromatic flavour.

kaffir lime leaves (bai magrood) sold fresh, dried or frozen; look like two glossy dark green leaves joined end to end, forming a round hourglass shape. Dried leaves are less potent, so double the number called for in a recipe if you substitute dried for fresh leaves.

kecap manis called sieu wan in Thai, sold here under this familiar Indonesian/Malaysian name; dark, thick, sweet soy sauce used in most South-East Asian cooking. Depending on the brand, the soy's sweetness is derived from the addition of either molasses or palm sugar when brewed.

lebanese cucumber medium-sized, slender and thin-skinned; this variety is also known as the european, hothouse or burpless cucumber.

lemon grass a tall, clumping, lemon-smelling and tasting, sharp-edged grass; the white lower part of the stem is used, finely chopped, in cooking.

mint

THAI (saranae) also known as marsh mint; similar to spearmint. Its somewhat thick round leaves are usually used raw, as a flavouring to be sprinkled over soups and salads.

VIETNAMESE not a mint at all, but a pungent and peppery narrow-leafed member of the buckwheat family. It is also known as cambodian mint, pak pai (Thailand), laksa leaf (Indonesia) or daun kesom (Singapore). It is a common ingredient in Thai foods, particularly soups, salads and stir-fries.

mushrooms

DRIED SHIITAKE also known as donko or dried chinese mushrooms; have a unique meaty flavour. Sold dried; rehydrate before use.

OYSTER also known as abalone; grey-white mushrooms shaped like a fan. Prized for their smooth texture and subtle, oyster-like flavour.

SHIITAKE also known as chinese black, forest or golden oak mushrooms; although cultivated, have the earthy taste of wild mushrooms. Large and fleshy, they are often used as a substitute for meat in some vegetarian dishes.

STRAW also known as paddy straw or grass mushrooms; seldom available fresh but easily found canned or dried in Asian grocery stores. A common ingredient in stir-fries, they have an intense, earthy flavour.

muslin inexpensive finely woven undyed cotton fabric. Can be used to strain stocks and sauces; coffee filter papers can be used instead.

noodles

BEAN THREAD (wun sen) made from extruded mung bean paste; also known as cellophane or glass noodles because they are transparent when cooked. White (not off-white like rice vermicelli), very delicate and fine; available dried in various-sized bundles. Must be soaked to soften before use; using them deep-fried requires no pre-soaking.

EGG (ba mee) also known as yellow noodles; made from wheat flour and eggs, sold fresh or dried. Range in size from fine strands to wide pieces as thick as a shoelace.

FRESH RICE also known as ho fun, pho or kway tiau, depending on the country of manufacture. The most common form of noodles used in Thailand can be purchased in various widths or in large sheets weighing about 500g which are cut into the width noodle desired. Chewy and pure white, they do not need pre-cooking before use.

FRIED crispy egg noodles packaged (commonly a 100g packet) already deep-fried.

HOKKIEN also known as stir-fry noodles; fresh wheat flour noodles resembling yellow-brown thick spaghetti. Need no pre-cooking before use.

RICE STICK (sen lek) also known as ho fun or kway teow; especially popular South-East Asian dried rice noodles. Come in different widths – thin used in soups, wide in stir-fries – but all should be soaked in hot water until soft. Sen lek, the traditional noodles used in pad thai, measure about 5mm in width before they are soaked.

VERMICELLI (sen mee) also known as mei fun or bee hoon. These are used throughout Asia in spring rolls and cold salads; similar to bean thread but longer and made with rice flour instead of mung bean starch. Before using, soak the dried noodles in hot water until soft (about 15 minutes), then boil them briefly (from 1 to 3 minutes) and rinse with hot water. You can also deep-fry the dried noodles until crunchy for use in coleslaw, chinese chicken salad, as a garnish or as a bed for sauces.

oil

PEANUT pressed from ground peanuts; most commonly used oil in Asian cooking because of its high smoke point (capacity to handle high heat without burning).

SESAME made from roasted crushed white sesame seeds; used as a flavouring rather than a cooking medium.

VEGETABLE any of a number of oils sourced from plants rather than animal fats.

onion

GREEN also known as scallion or (incorrectly) shallot; an immature onion picked before the bulb has formed, having a long, bright-green edible stalk.

SPRING crisp, narrow, green-leafed tops and a round, sweet white bulb larger than a green onion.

palm sugar (nam tan pip) also called jaggery, jawa or gula melaka; made from the sap of the sugar palm tree. Light brown to black in colour and usually sold in rock-hard cakes; substitute brown sugar if it is unavailable.

paprika ground dried red capsicum (bell pepper), available sweet or hot.

pattypan squash also known as crookneck or custard marrow pumpkin; a round, slightly flat summer squash being yellow to pale green in colour and having a scalloped edge. Harvested young, it has firm white flesh and a distinct flavour.

115

pickled garlic (kratiem dong) sweet and subtle young green bulb, packed in jars whole and unpeeled in a vinegar brine. Eaten as a snack in Thailand; can also be used in cooking or served as a condiment for noodle or rice dishes.

pickled green peppercorns (prik tai ahn) have a fresh herbal "green" flavour without being extremely pungent; early-harvested unripe pepper that needs to be dried or pickled to avoid fermentation. We used pickled thai green peppercorns, which are canned, still strung in clusters, but you can use an equivalent weight from a bottle of green peppercorns in brine.

pomelo (som-o) similar to grapefruit but sweeter, somewhat more conical in shape and slightly larger, about the size of a small coconut. The firm rind peels away easily and neatly, like a mandarin, and the segments are easy to separate.

preserved turnip (hua chai po or cu cai muoi on the label) is also called dried radish because of its similarity to daikon. Sold packaged whole or sliced, it is very salty and needs to be rinsed well before use.

rice

BLACK also known as purple rice because, while a deep charcoal in colour when raw, after cooking it turns a purplish-black colour. A medium-grain unmilled rice, with a white kernel under the black bran, it has a nutty, whole-grain flavour and is crunchy to the bite, similarly to wild rice.

GLUTINOUS also known as "sweet" rice or "sticky" rice; a short, fat grain having a chalky white centre. When cooked, it becomes soft and sticky, hence the name; requires fairly long soaking and steaming times.

THAI JASMINE recognised around the world as having a particular aromatic quality described as perfumed or floral; a long-grained white rice, it is sometimes substituted for basmati rice. Moist in texture, it clings together after cooking.

rice paper also known as banh trang; different to the edible fine glossy paper used in the making of biscuits and confectionery. Made from rice paste and stamped into rounds; stores well at room temperature. Dipped momentarily in water to become pliable, it makes good wrappers for fried foods, spring rolls and uncooked vegetables.

sambal oelek (also ulek or olek) Indonesian in origin; a salty paste made from ground red chillies and vinegar.

shallot

FRIED (homm jiew) are usually served as condiments on the Thai table or sprinkled over just-cooked dishes. Can be purchased packaged in jars or cellophane bags at all Asian grocery stores; once opened, they keep for months if stored tightly sealed. You can make your own by frying thinly sliced peeled shallots until golden-brown and crisp.

THAI PURPLE (homm) also called asian or pink shallots; used throughout South-East Asia, they are a member of the onion family but resemble garlic in that they grow in multiple-clove bulbs and are intensely flavoured. They are eaten fresh or deep-fried as a condiment.

shrimp paste (kapi) also known as trasi or blanchan; it is a strong-scented, very firm preserved paste made of salted dried shrimp. Used as a pungent flavouring in many South-East Asian soups and sauces. Must be chopped or sliced thinly, then wrapped in foil and roasted before use.

snake beans long (about 40cm), thin, round, fresh green beans, Asian in origin, with a taste similar to green or french beans. Used most frequently in stir-fries, they are also called yard-long beans because of their length.

soy sauce (sieu) made from fermented soy beans. Several variations are available in most supermarkets and Asian food stores; everyday Thai cooking calls for the use of two of them: sieu wan (see kecap manis) or sieu dum (dark soy).

star anise a star-shaped dried pod whose seeds have an astringent aniseed flavour; used to flavour stocks and marinades.

tamarind from the same family as various beans, the tamarind tree is native to tropical Africa and, more recently, South-East Asia, and can grow as high as 25 metres. The tree produces clusters of brown "hairy" pods (each of which is filled with seeds and a viscous pulp) that are dried and pressed into the blocks of tamarind found in Asian supermarkets. Gives a sweet-sour, slightly astringent taste to food. An important ingredient in Thai, Indian and other Asian cuisines, tamarind is used mainly as a souring agent in marinades, pastes, sauces and dressings. It is also used in the manufacturing of many curry pastes, ketchups and sauces.

tamarind concentrate (or paste) the commercial result of the distillation of tamarind juice into a condensed, compacted paste. Thick and purplish-black, it is ready to use, with no soaking or straining required; can be diluted with water according to taste. Use tamarind concentrate to add zing to sauces, chutneys and marinades.

tofu (tao hu) also known as bean curd, an off-white, custard-like product made from the "milk" of crushed soy beans; comes fresh as soft or firm, and processed as fried or pressed dried sheets. Leftover fresh tofu can be refrigerated in water (which is changed daily) up to 4 days. Silken tofu refers to the manufacturing method of straining the soy bean liquid through silk.

FIRM made by compressing bean curd to remove most of the water. Good used in stir-fries because it can be tossed without falling apart.

FRIED packaged pieces of soft bean curd which has been deep fried until the surface is brown and crusty and the inside almost dry.

SHEETS also known as dried bean curd skins or yuba; the sweet, stiff skin that forms on warm soy bean liquid as it cools. Needs to be reconstituted before being used.

SOFT delicate; does not hold its shape when drained or overhandled.

turmeric (kamin) a rhizome related to galangal and ginger; must be grated or pounded to release its somewhat acrid aroma and pungent flavour. Known for the golden colour it imparts to food, fresh turmeric can be substituted with the more common dried powder (use 2 teaspoons of ground turmeric plus 1 teaspoon of sugar for every 20g of fresh turmeric called for in a recipe).

vinegar

RICE WINE made from pure fermented rice with no flavourings added.

SEASONED RICE made from fermented rice, colourless and flavoured with sugar and salt.

wonton wrappers also known as wonton skins; made of flour, eggs and water, they come in varying thicknesses. Sold packaged in large amounts and found in the refrigerated sections of Asian grocery stores; gow gee, egg or spring roll pastry sheets can be substituted. We used thin wrappers measuring 12cm x 12cm in this book.

cooking term translations

English/Thai
barbecued, roasted **yang**
basil (holy) **kra pao**
basil (thai) **horapa**
beef **nuah**
chicken **gai**
coconut **kati**
coriander **pak chee**
crab **puu**
cup or wrap **hor**
curry pastes
   green **gaeng**
   keow wahn
   jungle **gaeng pak**
   massaman **gaeng**
   masaman
   panang **gaeng panaeng**
   red **gaeng ped**
   yellow **gaeng leuang**
deep-fried **tod**
deep-fried balls or patties
tod mun
duck **pet**
egg **khai**
finger-root (pickled) **ka
chai (dong)**
fish **pla**
fresh **sod**
fried garlic **kratiem jiew**
fried, stir-fried **pad**
galangal **ka**
garlic **kratiem**
ginger **khing**
kaffir lime **magrood**
lamb **kae**
lemon grass **takrai**
mushrooms **het**
mussels **hoy**
noodles
   cellophane/bean thread
   wun sen
   flat rice **kway tiau**
   fresh egg **ba mee**
   rice stick **sen lek**
   rice vermicelli **sen mee**
pork **muu**
prawn **goong**
pumpkin **fak tong**
rice **khao**
rice (sticky) **khao niaw**
salad **yum**
seafood **taleh**
shallot (fried) **homm jiew**
shallot (thai purple) **homm**
soup **tom**
sour **priaw**
squid **pla muk**
steamed **neung**
tofu **tao hu**
turmeric **kamin**
vegetable **pak**
vegetables, mixed
pak ruam

Thai/English
ba mee fresh egg noodles
dong pickled
gaeng keow wahn green
curry paste
gaeng leuang yellow
curry paste
gaeng pak jungle
curry paste
gaeng panaeng panang
curry paste
gaeng ped red
curry paste
gai chicken
goong prawn
het mushrooms
homm thai purple shallot
homm jiew fried shallot
hor cup or wrap
horapa thai basil
hoy mussels
ka galangal
ka chai finger-root
ka chai dong pickled
finger-root
ka dong pickled galangal
kae lamb
kamin turmeric
kati coconut
khai egg
khao rice
khao niaw sticky rice
khing ginger
khing dong
pickled ginger
kra pao holy basil
kratiem garlic
kratiem dong
pickled garlic
kratiem jiew fried garlic
kway tiau flat rice noodles
magrood kaffir lime
muu pork
nuah beef
pad fried, stir-fried
pak vegetable
pak ruam mixed
vegetables
pet duck
pla fish
pla muk squid
priaw sour
prik hot
puu crab
sen lek rice stick noodles
sen mee rice vermicelli
sod fresh
taleh seafood
tom soup
wun sen cellophane/bean
thread noodles
yang barbecued, roasted
yum salad

make your own stock

These recipes can be made up to 4 days ahead and kept, covered, in the refrigerator. Remove any fat from the surface after the cooled stock has been refrigerated overnight. If stock is to be kept longer, freeze it, divided into smaller quantities. All the recipes below make approximately 2.5 litres (10 cups) of stock.

Stock is also available in cans or cartons; stock cubes or powder can also be used. As a guide, 1 teaspoon of stock powder or 1 small crumbled stock cube mixed with 1 cup (250ml) water will result in a fairly strong stock. Be aware of the salt and fat content of these products.

beef stock

2kg meaty beef bones
2 medium onions (300g)
2 sticks celery, chopped
2 medium carrots (250g), chopped
3 bay leaves
2 teaspoons black peppercorns
5 litres (20 cups) water
3 litres (12 cups) water, extra

Place bones and unpeeled chopped onions in baking dish. Bake in hot oven about 1 hour or until well browned. Transfer bones and onions to large pan, add celery, carrots, bay leaves, peppercorns and the water, simmer, uncovered, 3 hours. Add extra water, simmer, uncovered, 1 hour; strain.

chicken stock

2kg chicken bones
2 medium onions (300g), chopped
2 sticks celery, chopped
2 medium carrots (250g), chopped
3 bay leaves
2 teaspoons black peppercorns
5 litres (20 cups) water

Combine all ingredients in large pan, simmer, uncovered, 2 hours; strain.

fish stock

1.5kg fish bones
3 litres (12 cups) water
1 medium onion (150g), chopped
2 sticks celery, chopped
2 bay leaves
1 teaspoon black peppercorns

Combine all ingredients in large pan, simmer, uncovered, 20 minutes; strain.

vegetable stock

2 large carrots (360g), chopped
2 large parsnips (360g), chopped
4 medium onions (600g), chopped
12 sticks celery, chopped
4 bay leaves
2 teaspoons black peppercorns
6 litres (24 cups) water

Combine all ingredients in large pan, simmer, uncovered, 1½ hours; strain.

index

facts + figures

Wherever you live, you'll be able to use our recipes with the help of these easy-to-follow conversions. While these conversions are approximate only, the difference between an exact and the approximate conversion of various liquid and dry measures is but minimal and will not affect your cooking results.

dry measures

metric	imperial
15g	½oz
30g	1oz
60g	2oz
90g	3oz
125g	4oz (¼lb)
155g	5oz
185g	6oz
220g	7oz
250g	8oz (½lb)
280g	9oz
315g	10oz
345g	11oz
375g	12oz (¾lb)
410g	13oz
440g	14oz
470g	15oz
500g	16oz (1lb)
750g	24oz (1½lb)
1kg	32oz (2lb)

oven temperatures

These oven temperatures are only a guide. Always check the manufacturer's manual.

	°C (Celsius)	°F (Fahrenheit)	Gas Mark
Very slow	120	250	1
Slow	150	300	2
Moderately slow	160	325	3
Moderate	180 — 190	350 — 375	4
Moderately hot	200 — 210	400 — 425	5
Hot	220 — 230	450 — 475	6
Very hot	240 — 250	500 — 525	7

liquid measures

metric	imperial
30ml	1 fluid oz
60ml	2 fluid oz
100ml	3 fluid oz
125ml	4 fluid oz
150ml	5 fluid oz (¼ pint/1 gill)
190ml	6 fluid oz
250ml	8 fluid oz
300ml	10 fluid oz (½ pint)
500ml	16 fluid oz
600ml	20 fluid oz (1 pint)
1000ml (1 litre)	1¾ pints

helpful measures

metric	imperial
3mm	⅛in
6mm	¼in
1cm	½in
2cm	¾in
2.5cm	1in
5cm	2in
6cm	2½in
8cm	3in
10cm	4in
13cm	5in
15cm	6in
18cm	7in
20cm	8in
23cm	9in
25cm	10in
28cm	11in
30cm	12in (1ft)

measuring equipment

The difference between one country's measuring cups and another's is, at most, within a 2 or 3 teaspoon variance. (For the record, 1 Australian metric measuring cup holds approximately 250ml.) The most accurate way of measuring dry ingredients is to weigh them. When measuring liquids, use a clear glass or plastic jug with the metric markings. (One Australian metric tablespoon holds 20ml; one Australian metric teaspoon holds 5ml.)

If you would like to purchase *The Australian Women's Weekly* Test Kitchen's metric measuring cups and spoons (as approved by Standards Australia), turn to page 120 for details and order coupon. You will receive:

- a graduated set of four cups for measuring dry ingredients, with sizes marked on the cups.
- a graduated set of four spoons for measuring dry and liquid ingredients, with amounts marked on the spoons.

Note: North America, NZ and the UK use 15ml tablespoons. All cup and spoon measurements are level.

We use large eggs having an average weight of 60g.

how to measure

When using graduated metric measuring cups, shake dry ingredients loosely into the appropriate cup. Do not tap the cup on a bench or tightly pack the ingredients unless directed to do so. Level top of measuring cups and measuring spoons with a knife. When measuring liquids, place a clear glass or plastic jug with metric markings on a flat surface to check accuracy at eye level.

Looking after **your interest...**

Keep your ACP cookbooks clean, tidy and within easy reach with slipcovers designed to hold up to 12 books. Plus you can follow our recipes perfectly with a set of accurate measuring cups and spoons, as used by *The Australian Women's Weekly* Test Kitchen.

To order

Mail or fax Photocopy and complete the coupon below and post to ACP Books Reader Offer, ACP Publishing, GPO Box 4967, Sydney NSW 2001, or fax to (02) 9267 4967.

Phone Have your credit card details ready, then phone 136 116 (Mon-Fri, 8.00am-6.00pm; Sat, 8.00am-6.00pm).

Price

Book Holder

Australia: $13.10 (incl. GST).
Elsewhere: $A21.95.

Metric Measuring Set

Australia: $6.50 (incl. GST).
New Zealand: $A8.00.
Elsewhere: $A9.95.

Prices include postage and handling. This offer is available in all countries.

Payment

Australian residents

We accept the credit cards listed on the coupon, money orders and cheques.

Overseas residents

We accept the credit cards listed on the coupon, drafts in $A drawn on an Australian bank, and also British, New Zealand and U.S. cheques in the currency of the country of issue. Credit card charges are at the exchange rate current at the time of payment.

Test Kitchen Staff
Food director *Pamela Clark*
Food editor *Karen Hammial*
Assistant food editor *Amira Ibram*
Test Kitchen manager *Kimberley Coverdale*
Senior home economist *Kellie Ann*
Home economists *Sammie Coryton, Kelly Cruickshanks, Cathie Lonnie, Christina Martignago, Jeanette Seamons, Alison Webb*
Editorial coordinator *Laura O'Brien*

ACP Books Staff
Editorial director *Susan Tomnay*
Creative director *Hieu Chi Nguyen*
Senior editor *Lynda Wilton*
Designer *Hieu Chi Nguyen*
Studio manager *Caryl Wiggins*
Editorial coordinator *Holly van Oyen*
Editorial assistant *Lana Meldrum*
Publishing manager (sales) *Brian Cearnes*
Publishing manager (rights & new projects) *Jane Hazell*
Brand manager *Donna Gianniotis*
Pre-press *Harry Palmer*
Production manager *Carol Currie*
Business manager *Sally Lees*
Chief executive officer *John Alexander*
Group publisher *Jill Baker*
Publisher *Sue Wannan*

Produced by ACP Books, Sydney.
Printed by Dai Nippon Printing in Korea.
Published by ACP Publishing Pty Limited, 54 Park St, Sydney; GPO Box 4088, Sydney, NSW 1028.
Ph: (02) 9282 8618 Fax: (02) 9267 9438.
acpbooks@acp.com.au
www.acpbooks.com.au
To order books, phone 136 116.
Send recipe enquiries to:
recipeenquiries@acp.com.au
AUSTRALIA: Distributed by Network Services GPO Box 4088, Sydney, NSW 1028.
Ph: (02) 9282 8777 Fax: (02) 9264 3278.
UNITED KINGDOM: Distributed by Australian Consolidated Press (UK), Moulton Park Business Centre, Red House Rd, Moulton Park, Northampton, NN3 6AQ.
Ph: (01604) 497 531 Fax: (01604) 497 533
acpukltd@aol.com
CANADA: Distributed by Whitecap Books Ltd, 351 Lynn Ave, North Vancouver, BC, V7J 2C4.
Ph: (604) 980 9852 Fax: (604) 980 8197
customerservice@whitecap.ca
www.whitecap.ca
NEW ZEALAND: Distributed by Netlink Distribution Company, ACP Media Centre, Cnr Fanshawe and Beaumont Streets, Westhaven, Auckland.
PO Box 47906, Ponsonby, Auckland, NZ.
Ph: (9) 366 9966 ask@ndcnz.co.nz

Clark, Pamela.
The Australian Women's Weekly Beginners Thai.

Includes index.
ISBN 1 86396 299 9
1. Cookery, Thai. I. Title. II. Title: Beginners Thai. III. Title: Australian Women's Weekly.
641.59593

© ACP Publishing Pty Limited 2003
ABN 18 053 273 546

First published 2003.

The publishers would like to thank the following for props used in photography:
Aneka Collection, Newtown, NSW
Cambodia House, Paddington, NSW
Mark Conway, Paddington, NSW
Mosmania, Mosman, NSW
Village Living, Avalon, NSW.

Photocopy and complete coupon below

☐ **Book Holder**

☐ **Metric Measuring Set**
   Please indicate number(s) required.

Mr/Mrs/Ms _____

Address _____

_____

Postcode _____ Country _____

Ph: Business hours (   ) _____

I enclose my cheque/money order for $ _____ payable to ACP Publishing.

OR: please charge my

☐ Bankcard   ☐ Visa   ☐ Mastercard

☐ Diners Club   ☐ American Express

Card number

Expiry date ____ /____

Cardholder's signature _____

Please allow up to 30 days delivery within Australia.
Allow up to 6 weeks for overseas deliveries.
Both offers expire 31/12/03. HLBT03